Making
Women
Matter

Making Women Matter

The Role of the United Nations

By Hilkka Pietilä
and Jeanne Vickers

Zed Books

Making Women Matter was first published by Zed Books Ltd,
57 Caledonian Road, London N1 9BU, UK, and 171 First Avenue,
Atlantic Highlands, New Jersey 07716, USA, in association with
The United Nations International Research and Training Institute
for Women (INSTRAW) and the United Nations Non-Governmental
Liaison Service, Geneva, in 1990.

Cover designed by Andrew Corbett.
Printed and bound in the United Kingdom
by Biddles Ltd, Guildford and King's Lynn.

UK CIP data is available from the British Library
US CIP data is available from the Library of Congress

ISBN 0-86232-968-X
ISBN 0-86232-969-8 Pbk

Contents

Annexes:

1. Convention on the Elimination of All Forms of Discrimination Against Women (full text)

2. Selected Guidelines and Checklists for Women in Development (INSTRAW)

3. Organizations that have agreed to implement the System-wide
   Medium-term Plan for Women and Development

4. United Nations World Conferences 1970-1988

5. How to prepare a resolution for a UN Conference

6. Relevant International Instruments

7. Where to ask for more information

Foreword

From the time of its inception, the United Nations has addressed the issues related to the status of women through the work of its competent organs, the Commission on the Status of Women, the Economic and Social Council and the General Assembly. Guided by the UN Charter and its emphasis on "the dignity and worth of the human person and the equal rights of men and women", United Nations bodies and agencies have been acting for the advancement of women as part of their global commitment to peace and disarmament, the promotion of human rights and social and economic development.

Using the history of UN involvement in these issues, *Making Women Matter* — the Role of the United Nations — shows how, over a remarkably short period of time, the approach to women's issues, originally based on the adoption and implementation of legal instruments for equal rights, has broadened to include all the dimensions and challenges of women's status in the face of multiple development constraints.

One of the most important achievements of the UN Decade for Women (1976-85) was the establishment of interrelationships between development processes and the position of women. *Making Women Matter* analyses how the Decade, and subsequent efforts, have resulted in a large body of innovative concepts and strategies. It also shows how action on behalf of, and indeed by, women, and the full recognition of their role, are essential components of the struggle to overcome the development impediments which continue to deprive entire populations — women, men and their children — of real improvements in their living conditions. As the End-Decade Conference held in Nairobi in 1985 made abundantly clear, the original objectives of the Decade are no less relevant to today's and tomorrow's action. The review process undertaken for that conference, which looked at the achievements as well as at the obstacles, also revealed the magnitude of the task facing the world community if the Forward-looking Strategies are to be implemented by the year 2000.

This book is about how the perceptions of women, their performance and their contributions, have changed — irreversibly. To understand how this came about, it is important to recognize the catalytic role played by the United Nations which, as in other periods of change, was the political forum where much of the discussion was held and many of the decisions taken.

The UN International Research and Training Institute for the Advancement of Women (INSTRAW) and the UN Non-Governmental Liaison Service (UN-NGLS) are pleased to present this joint publication, which they believe will provide essential information to non-governmental organizations and to the public at large. The opinions expressed therein are those of the authors, who have worked tirelessly in support of the United Nations.

Writing from a non-governmental perspective, Hilkka Pietilä sifted a large volume of reports and studies and selected the documents which she considered pertinent to the issue. She and the editorial talent of Jeanne Vickers have brought to the readers the story of how women have made history, of how much the world needs to continue to change for women to receive their equal share of progress, and of the role the UN plays in promoting recognition of the fact that women do, indeed, matter.

UN International Research and Training Institute for the Advancement of Women (INSTRAW), Santo Domingo, Dominican Republic

UN Non-Governmental Liaison Service (NGLS), Geneva, Switzerland

Authors' Preface

Over the years, issues concerning and of interest to women have taken on new forms and received varying treatment by the United Nations System and its Specialised Agencies. The principle of the equality of men and women was already recognised in 1945, in the United Nations Charter, and subsequently again in the Universal Declaration of Human Rights.

But in the 1950's and 1960's women's issues, seen mainly within the context of human rights, were discussed only in the Commission on the Status of Women and the Third Committee of the UN General Assembly, which deals with social and humanitarian matters.

In the 1970's, the perspective changed decisively, and the key role of women, especially in connection with efforts to relieve or solve problems in the fields of population and food issues, became more generally recognized. Although this was not yet fully perceived when the International Development Strategy for the UN's Second Development Decade was drafted at the end of the 1960's, by 1972 the decision had been taken to declare 1975 International Women's Year. Throughout the 1970's women's issues came to the fore in several world conferences convened by the UN to study and adopt specific plans of action for the solution of major problems of world development.

Thus, it was not until the 1970's that the UN agenda really started specifically to address the concerns of the female half of humankind. In the UN's earlier decades they had been seen as objects, for whose protection and rights recommendations were made and conventions enacted. In the

1970's the formula was to "integrate women into development"; characteristically, they were seen as resources and their contributions were sought to enhance the development process and to make it more efficient. For this purpose it was necessary to improve the status, nutrition, health and education of women. It was often claimed to be "a waste of human resources" if women were not fully integrated into development efforts. Their dignity and rights were not yet seen as a cause in its own right. The perennial nature of their contribution to the well-being of each country's population was still unrecognized within the development context.

Then, in the International Development Strategy for the UN's Third Development Decade (the 1980's), a trend towards seeing women as equals, "as agents and beneficiaries in all sectors and at all levels of the development process", finally emerges. And the year 1985 became a turning point in the history of women's issues in the UN System.

In that year the World Conference to Review and Appraise the Achievements of the UN Decade for Women took place in Nairobi, and adopted unanimously the Forward-looking Strategies for the Advancement of Women Towards the Year 2000. These Strategies specifically recognize women as "intellectuals, policy-makers, planners and contributors, and beneficiaries of development", and obligate both member governments and the United Nations System to implement the Strategies in practice. When this is finally the case, we shall be able to say that the UN System is living up to its Charter by recognizing the "other half" of humanity as equals.

This book takes as its starting point the results and impact of the Nairobi Conference. Then we review the process which led to that conference and constitutes the background of its outcome, and the decisions and programmes later adopted in the UN System in order to implement its obligations. Finally, we look at future perspectives for women's participation and influence in the international community, women's role in development and within the United Nations System, and make proposals for the full and appropriate recognition of the Nairobi FLS by the international community as it works towards the year 2000.

* * *

We should like to express our gratitude to those who have rewarded our work as active observers of, and participants in, UN activities for more than thirty years by entrusting us with the task of writing this book. It has given us an opportunity to study the history of women's issues in the UN System even more thoroughly, and to share the experiences and insights gained over the years in our work as Secretary-General of the Finnish United Nations Association and as UNICEF's Development Education Officer with those who read this book and are interested in the advancement of women worldwide.

Cooperation between the UN International Research and Training Institute for the Advancement of Women (INSTRAW) and the United Nations Non-Governmental Liaison Service in Geneva in the production of this book has allowed us to write from the NGO viewpoint — the most familiar to us — implying comment and constructive criticism of the work of the UN System and the issues discussed. Our personal involvement in the international women's movement and women's research explains why the text may reflect enthusiasm and belief in the strength and quality of the contribution that women can make to the efforts of the UN System in bringing about a better future for humanity as a whole.

Our very warm personal thanks go to Dr. Krishna Patel of INSTRAW and to Thierry Lemaresquier of UN/NGLS, who have encouraged and helped us with great patience and whose cooperation has enabled this book to be published.

Hilkka Pietilä	**Jeanne Vickers**
Helsinki, 1 January 1990	Geneva

1.
Towards New Millennia:
Forward from Nairobi

What happened in Nairobi in 1985?

The past few decades have seen a new era unfolding, and the culmination of an important development in the history of humanity. From the great hopes and wishful, barely articulated expectations of the Mexico City conference which opened the *United Nations Decade for Women* in 1975, the women of the world have developed their aspirations to the point at which they became well-defined action plans in Nairobi. Within a decade a new self-confidence and common sense of purpose emerged among women everywhere as they reached out to each other across frontiers. Global sisterhood is becoming a reality. Women have found new bonds between themselves, connecting them in ways they had never dreamed of, and new networks are being created through which they can work together.

Such is the result of the United Nations Decade for Women. The process which was maturing at the beginning of the 1970s made a leap forward in Mexico City in 1975, underwent a mid-term stocktaking in Copenhagen in 1980, and unfolded itself fully at the World Conference in Nairobi in mid-1985.

In fact, there were two conferences, partly parallel, which took place in Nairobi: the United Nations World Conference to Review and Appraise the Achievements of the UN Decade for Women, 15-26 July 1985; and the Non-Governmental World Conference of Women, *Forum '85*, 10-19 July 1985. Each had been carefully prepared beforehand, by the UN on the one hand and by non-governmental organizations

(NGOs) on the other, utilising to the full the experiences of the Mexico and Copenhagen conferences. Preparations were also undertaken in good time in UN member countries, where much work was done during the preceding several years.

NGO Forum '85

A special planning committee for NGO activities in connection with the World Conference was established almost two years ahead by the Conference of NGOs in New York (known as CONGO), to prepare both for activities on the spot in Nairobi and on the part of interested NGOs around the world. These NGOs were already on the alert, the experiences in Mexico City and Copenhagen having already given birth to great expectations. Thousands of women were planning to participate in Nairobi.

They were also alert to the need to follow and lobby the preparations of their governments, having learned from previous experience that it is extremely difficult to influence intergovernmental decisions on the spot during a world conference. Preferably it must be done beforehand in each country, by women expressing their wishes and suggestions to the appropriate governmental bodies. And in order to make their efforts coherent it was necessary for women to coordinate their activities internationally as well, so that the same suggestions and pressures were applied in parallel in as many countries as possible.

Links established at previous NGO conferences now helped groups and organizations wanting to act on specific issues to reach each other. Women's groups, non-governmental organizations, researchers, women's movements and campaigners in a large number of countries were thus both lobbying their own governmental preparations and preparing to bring their programmes and contributions to Nairobi. A great many coordinating and preparatory meetings were held, both nationally and internationally, during the two years before the Nairobi Conference.

The NGOs' *IWY Tribune* in Mexico City in 1975, and the *NGO Forum* in Copenhagen in 1980, were the biggest NGO

conferences so far to meet in parallel with UN world conferences. Nairobi's *Forum '85* doubled in size, with more than
14,000 women attending from over 150 countries according to
official records. Unofficial sources estimate that the real
number, including all those involved in organising and
managing the practical arrangements in the various facilities and locations, was at least 16,000. *Forum '85* was a World
Conference of Women in the real sense of the definition, a
gathering of women from all over the world without equal
in the past.

It was also like a women's world fair in the richness of its
arts and handicrafts, its inventions and inspirations, its research and achievements. Above all, it was a joyful union of
sisterhood, experiencing the sense of power in working together hand-in-hand, seeing eye-to-eye. The strength and
dignity of African women made an unforgettable impression (upon us, Europeans). Some 125 workshops and meetings were scheduled each day — about 1,200 altogether —
and there was a constant flow of improvised gatherings, discussions, group meetings of all kinds and in all places, on
the green lawns of the Nairobi University campus, under the
trees here and there, in the Peace tent, in hotels and dormi-
tories — wherever space was available.

One of the characteristic features of the Forum was that
women were actively doing things, organizing, presenting,
participating, discussing, and also dancing, singing and
performing, not just passively sitting and listening as in so
many conferences in general. There were no authoritarian
speakers and lecturers, all were authorities in being women
and knowing the lives of women, so there was a constant exchange of views, experiences and opinion, and a sharing of
research and knowledge.

It is impossible to give a comprehensive picture of
Forum '85. Still, reflections and impressions are as good a
record of this enormous exercise in the empowerment of
women at the global level. Women returned home stronger
than before, and brought with them the experience of what
sisterhood is all about. All this gave support also to the
official UN Conference, not so much in the form of
resolutions or direct messages but in the form of spirit and

influence on the minds of those official delegates who came early in order to attend the Forum.

There are naturally no official records with regard to this unofficial women's world conference in Nairobi, but with the help of Dame Nita Barrow, Convenor, and Virginia Hazzard, Coordinator of the NGO Planning Commitee, the story of the Forum has been told in a report entitled *For the Record ... Forum '85.*[1]

There was a feeling in the Forum that this kind of world conference of women should, whenever possible, be organized independently and irrespectively of the United Nations or intergovernmental events. While at that time only a dream in the minds of many, the idea is alive and evolving.

In the summer of 1987 a *World Congress of Women* was organized in Moscow by the Women's International Democratic Federation, bringing together more than 3,000 women from over the world and reviving the spirit of Nairobi. In summer 1988 a Nordic Women's *Forum '88* was organized in Oslo, Norway, and attended by about 10,000 women, primarily from the Nordic countries but also from other parts of the world. In between these two there have been smaller events, such as the *Third Interdisciplinary Congress on Women* in Dublin, 1987, the *Global Peace International Women's Conference* in Dallas in 1988, and many others in which the spirit of the global women's movement has recalled the atmosphere and sense of sisterhood which was so evident in Nairobi.

All this is manifested in the emerging, subtle strength of the international women's movement, the impetus behind these events. And rapidly evolving feminist research both gives evidence of, and adds to, the growing awareness among women everywhere.

The World Conference of the UN Decade for Women, Nairobi

The decision taken at the Mid-Decade World Conference in Copenhagen, 1980, "to convene in 1985, at the conclusion of the Decade, a World Conference to review and appraise the achievements of the United Nations Decade for Women", had as its purpose:

— the critical review and appraisal of progress achieved and obstacles encountered in attaining the goals and objectives of the UN Decade for Women;

— the adoption of forward-looking strategies of implementation for the advancement of women for the period up to the year 2000.

Preparations for this official intergovernmental conference consisted of two major surveys: the World Survey on the Role of Women in Development,[2] and the Review and Appraisal of progress achieved and obstacles encountered at the national level in the realization of the goals and objectives of the United Nations Decade for Women.[3] The first will be presented in the following chapter. The second was based on replies by governments to an extensive questionnaire, which give a great deal of information about what really had happened in UN member countries during the Decade.

The point of departure for both of these assessment processes was, naturally, the 1975 World Plan of Action adopted in Mexico to set the goals and objectives for the whole Decade, as well as the Programme of Action for the Second Half of the Decade adopted in Copenhagen in 1980. There was also the International Development Strategy for the Third UN Development Decade, adopted in 1980, which reaffirmed the principles of the World Plan of Action and the recommendations of the Copenhagen World Conference. In fact, the World Survey on the Role of Women in Development is directly related to the IDS and thus reviews and assesses development from the woman's point of view beyond the World Plan of Action, as we shall see in the following chapter.

All this sounds like a very bureaucratic procedure, but in reality this kind of intergovernmental exercise — responding to UN questionnaires and preparing for world conferences — is a mechanism for making governments implement the plans and recommendations put forward in UN conferences. In order to have something to report in the questionnaire, governments need to have done something in practice. For example, in Finland the World Plan of Action for the Implementation of the Objectives of the IWY led to preparation of a government equality programme for 1980-

1985, which required that each Ministry plan ways and means of promoting equality between men and women and set up a systematic programme for its field of administration. This was approved by the government in the spring of 1980, so that the Finnish delegation was able to report on it in Copenhagen.

World Conferences have also speeded up ratification of the Convention on the Elimination of All Forms of Discrimination Against Women. They created pressure on governments (e.g. in Finland) to make the necessary changes in legislation in order to be able to ratify the Convention. Such processes have taken place in many countries, and the number of ratifications has grown very rapidly. In less than ten years from its adoption in 1979, 96 countries had already ratified it as of March 1989.

But the task of the Nairobi Conference was not only to review and appraise what had been achieved, what had not been achieved, and why not; its primary task was to draw conclusions about the experiences and obstacles encountered in the attainment of the goals of the UNDW, and to prepare Forward-looking Strategies for the Advancement of Women for the period up to the year 2000.

And it was clear from all the evaluations and assessments that the goals and objectives of the UNDW had been achieved only partly during the Decade; a lot remained to be achieved in future years. So while there was not that much need to redefine the goals and objectives, it was necessary to develop further the strategies for overcoming the obstacles to the achievement of those goals.

One of the major achievements of the Decade was that the situation of the world's women was better mapped than ever before. An enormous amount of new information was collected; figures and statistics were becoming more accurate, with more and more of them giving figures separately for men and women, etc. The pivotal role of women in issues such as population and food was perceived, and some of the "invisibilities" started to be visualized. The whole story of so-called development from the woman's point of view began to be revealed, a story which is documented in the World Survey on the Role of Women in Development, in *DAWN-Report* and in countless other reports and stories. And after all, "during this period, women's consciousness and expectations have been raised, and it is important that this momentum should not be lost, regardless of the poor performance of the world economy".

If participation in Forum '85 was overwhelming, so was the number of delegates to the World Conference — about one-third more than in previous conferences of the UNDW. There were more than 2,000 delegates from 157 countries, and several hundred representatives of NGOs in consultative status to the United Nations, attending the official World Conference.

Notes

[1] *For the Record ... Forum '85. The Non-Governmental World Meeting for Women,* Nairobi, Kenya. Prepared by Caroline Pezzullo for the NGO Planning Committee. Available from International Women's Tribune Center, 777 United Nations Plaza, New York, NY 10017.

[2] *The World Survey on the Role of Women in Development.* United Nations, New York, 1986. A/CONF.116/4/Rev.1, Sales No. E.86.IV.3.

[3] *Review and appraisal of progress achieved and obstacles encountered at the national level in the realization of the goals and objectives of the United Nations Decade or Women: Equality, Development and Peace.* Report of the Secretary-General. A/CONF.116/5 and Addenda 1-14. Also A/CONF.116/28, Rev.1, Sales No. E.85.IV.10.

2.
Development From
Women's Point of View

First time in history

One outcome of the United Nations Decade for Women and the World Conferences in Mexico City and Copenhagen was the decision of the General Assembly in December 1980 to request the Secretary-General to prepare an interdisciplinary and multisectoral World Survey on the role of women in overall development. The task was further defined in the following year by the 36th Session of the General Assembly, when it was stipulated that "the survey should analyse the role of women in relation to the key developmental issues as envisaged in the International Development Strategy for the Third United Nations Development Decade, focusing in particular on trade, agriculture, industry, energy, money and finance, and science and technology."

This recommendation was a decisive step forward in the way in which the women's aspect in development has been perceived. At the Copenhagen Conference in 1980 the approach was still to focus primarily on health, education and employment as major concerns for women. Now it was realized that there is a major concern for women in all key development issues, both at macro- and micro-level. The question still remains whether even this approach will cover all aspects of major importance for women.

In any event, this was a turning point in the history of women's issues in the UN System. Until now the spotlight had been turned on women when the point of women's concerns was made. Now the spotlight was on the major issues, but as if women themselves were focusing it so that those aspects which particularly concern women could also be seen. Now women were turning the spotlight, instead of being only its focus.

The World Survey on the Role of Women in Development[1]

It was also decided in 1983 that the World Survey should constitute one of the basic documents for the 1985 World Conference in Nairobi. It was also to be different from any previous studies in two ways: it would look at development globally from the woman's point of view, in industrialized as well as developing countries, and it would be intersectoral or interagency so as to cover the scope of the whole UN system and interrelate the findings across the sectoral borders. All previous development reports had focused on the situation of women in developing countries only — as if there were no women's concerns at all in the development of industrialized countries!

The intersectoral structure of the Survey meant that it was prepared in collaboration with various organs and agencies of the UN System. The work was directed by the Department of International Economic and Social Affairs (DIESA), with FAO, UNIDO, UNCSTD and INSTRAW[2] contributing their own chapters.

According to the General Assembly's instructions the Survey was to cover:

(a) the present role of women as active agents of development in each sector.

(b) an assessment of the benefits accruing to women as a result of their participation in development, namely income, conditions of work and decision-making.

(c) ways and means of improving women's role as agents and beneficiaries of development at the national, regional and international levels.

(d) the potential impact of such improvements on the achievement of overall development goals.

The Survey was not easy to produce. From the beginning the work was handicapped by the inadequacy of data and statistics on a global scale. From many countries statistics are not available, and when they are they may not be comparable. A constant major problem is the lack of statistical differentiation between men and women, although this has improved in recent decades. Evidence available on such indicators of benefits as income, access to resources, decision-making power and prestige is scant.

The mere definitions are not explicit; what constitutes development or benefits varies from culture to culture. The relationship between economic growth, development and an overall improved standard of living is by no means automatic. While in the long-term both women and men will benefit from development if it ensures equity, improvement of life and peace, it is questionable whether all women will benefit in the short and medium terms, which were the time perspectives of the Survey.

The main shortcoming of all global economic statistics from women's point of view is, without doubt, the invisibility of the unpaid labour in households and the informal and agricultural sectors, a major part of which, in all countries, is performed by women.

This problem was taken up right at the beginning of the Survey, because the exclusion of unpaid labour from all the statistics distorts the assessment of women's contribution to economic development and the well-being of their countries. So the whole Survey on the role of women in development — like other surveys at the present time — suffers from this profound inadequacy, which must be kept in mind throughout.

In order to help us rectify our thinking in this respect, the World Survey discusses quite substantively the importance of unpaid labour in various sectors of life. Most significant, and usually totally blurred, is domestic work which, in reality, has an immeasurable economic importance. "Being unpaid labour for the most part, it lowers the cost of reproduction of the labour force and subsidizes male paid labour; as a result, it is a powerful factor in the accumulation of capital in many countries at all levels of development", says the Survey.

In addition the so-called informal sector, in agriculture and trade, comprises a significant amount of unregistered labour. In all these fields women's contribution is significant but grossly underestimated. A major part of trading lies within the informal labour sector that has historically been one of the least recognised statistically, for men as well as for women. The informal labour market also covers a huge variety of occupations and skills. Most of these contributions by women in developing countries are not included in any statistics either.

In the following review of the content of the World Survey it is possible only to highlight some of the most interesting findings, and pinpoint especially what is particularly important for a new perspective on women's role in development. Hopefully these passages can create sufficient interest for the reader to seek the actual source of information.

Industry

A typical transformation in world industry in recent decades has been the redeployment of labour-intensive production from developed to developing countries, particularly in such sectors as textiles, clothing, food processing, pharmaceuticals, electronics assembly and, generally, light consumer goods. This process has had an important and irreversible impact on the rapid expansion of wage employment of women in general, and on industrial employment in particular. Between 1960 and 1980 the total number of women in the labour force worldwide increased 39% but the percentage of women in industry rose by 104%.

Many developing country governments have even used an "excessive" supply of docile, dexterous and adaptable women workers as an incentive and advantage for foreign corporations to locate their production in those countries. In addition they have provided concrete economic incentives in the form of tax holidays, investment credits, creation of export-processing zones (EPZs) with appropriate infrastructure for transnational corporations, etc. For the EPZs they have also provided special legislation which effectively prevents the organization of labour unions or, for example, the enforcement of minimum wage levels.

As a consequence, the proportion of women workers in many EPZs soon exceeded 80%. They were young, unmarried and childless, in the beginning most of them between the ages of 15 and 25. Many firms refused to hire married women and even dismissed female employees who married. Meanwhile the total absence of any support services for the domestic duties of women made it practically impossible for them to continue working after marriage.

Traditionally, women have been considered only supplementary earners. Therefore they lack bargaining power, and this makes them cheaper to hire and easier to fire than men. One more typical aspect is that the skills required from women in simple mechanical work are acquired in unremunerated domestic work, which therefore need not be counted in assessment of pay levels.

Migration of women from the countryside to industrial work is part of the urbanization process, which is accompanied by industrialization and transformation to a monetized economy. This may release women from arduous work in the subsistence economy, and from economic dependence on traditional families. But in the cities, as recent immigrants, they usually find work primarily only in unstable service activities and marginal trading. The modern industrial sector is largely inaccessible to women except in the export processing zones; most of the other industrial jobs go to men.

The foreign, transnational industry is also an extremely unstable employer. It is very sensitive to short-term fluctuations in demand, and production is easily closed or transferred to another country and employees laid off. Since women are placed primarily in the subordinate, lowest-paid jobs at the bottom of the pay structure, they are also the first to be fired. It is typical for women's work in EPZs to be limited to a few years and to the most mechanical activities, such as assembly work.

One more aspect of the industrialization process is particularly significant for women. Large-scale modern industrial production is often geared towards the production of products similar to those women have been producing in traditional handicraft manufacture. Such industrial production competes with traditional production, which is forced out of the market in no time and thus makes the traditional earnings of women impossible. They don't have many options left, and as an overall result they are even further squeezed. They become ever more easy pawns of unscrupulous enterprises.

The World Survey makes numerous recommendations for the alleviation of the detrimental effects of the industrialization process on women, and the improvement and promotion of women's opportunities to benefit from industrial progress:

— The paramount issue is naturally the education and training of women. Both general education and vocational training need to be extended, and girls' access to them assured. The education gap between boys and girls should be abolished, and girls should be especially encouraged to proceed into higher learning and technical and entrepreneurial training.

— Women in industry should be provided with on-the-job training in more transferable skills, which they could use in local enterprises later on.

— Governments should, through various measures, support and promote small-scale production in the informal sector, at least in proportion to their support for large-scale production.

— Work in the informal sector should be well-organized, e.g. through establishment of cooperatives, to make the best use of available resources and to produce goods for which there is a reliable and steady demand.

— Women as entrepreneurs and self-employed workers should be assisted by training in skills for running small businesses, and by providing them with credit facilities, access to technical advice and assistance, and information on market conditions, demand trends, etc.

— The informal sector should be structurally expanded and improved, because it leads to greater participation of women in industrial activities.

Finally, the Survey assesses the potential impact of the improvement of women's position in the industrial process on the achievement of overall development goals.

Improving the situation of women in industry is not simply a matter of women's welfare and greater equity. Providing more resources to traditional, informal sectors of the economy will increase output and productivity in domestic consumer goods industries, raising real income and hence demand for these goods. The ultimate result will thus be, in the best case, more economic self-reliance and reduced dependence on imports.

Raising the level of women's earnings also entails a redistribution of income in favour of the least-paid workers, and especially women-headed households, which are many and usually the poorest in the society. "The improvement of women's position and attack on poverty are closely allied", says the Survey.

Agriculture

In the field of agriculture the ordinary statistics on women's work have been most misleading, giving a totally false picture of the situation. This is due not only to a macro and mechanical approach in the collection of information for statistics, but also to many cultural and other factors which make people themselves perceive and report their situation in an unrealistic manner. The consequences of incorrect perceptions of reality have been seen on the world scale in recent decades, when efforts to alleviate food problems have failed.

The World Survey rectifies a lot of these misperceptions. It goes through many comparisons between official national statistics and in-depth community level studies. The discrepancies between national census statistics and micro-studies seem to be the most glaring for the Latin America, Middle East and North Africa regions. There are two main reasons for such discrepancies: (a) considerable under-estimates of rural women who are economically active as unpaid family workers, and (b) the fact that livestock care, usually the domain of women, is rarely considered an agricultural economic activity.

One example is Egypt, where 1970 national statistics showed that women represented only 3.6% of the agricultural labour force. An in-depth interview-study revealed that, in lower Egypt, half of the wives ploughed and levelled the land, and between 55-70% participated in important agricultural production activities. About three-quarters of Egyptian wives engaged in milking and poultry activities. In fact, the data showed that rural households in Egypt, as in most other developing countries, can best be conceptualized as small rural enterprises where farming systems operated by husbands and wives together usually occupy the central position, unless the households are landless.

The 1972 Peruvian census showed 2.6% of rural women to be economically active in Cajamarca department agriculture. An interview-study showed that women participated in agricultural field work in 86% of all households. And if one considers the total labour input (male and female) in all farm activity (including processing, marketing and animal care), the smallholder agriculture in the area qualifies as a female farming system, states the Survey. The cardinal error of national statistics seems to be due — according to the researchers — to deep-rooted patriarchal values that make men and women reluctant to report women's actual participation.

In largely Moslem Asian countries (e.g. Pakistan and Bangladesh) women's agricultural contribution also remains practically invisible. For example, in the rice and cotton villages of Pakistan women spend 40-50% of their time in agricultural work with livestock-rearing, in addition to constituting 29% of rice production and 24% of cotton production. Still to be added to the contributions of women to agricultural production activities are kitchen gardening, cleaning and drying the farm produce for storage, making clay storage "bins", and preparing and carrying the meals, tea etc. to men working in the fields.

These examples seem to indicate that we have to rectify the generally adopted notions about the big variations in women's participation in agricultural production between North Africa and sub-Saharan Africa, and between Africa and Southern Asia. Maybe the long-believed theory of the importance of plough and hoe, as the main instruments in agriculture, being a dividing factor between regions with respect to the distribution of labour between men and women needs to be revised?

The Survey gives much emphasis to the rectification of statistics and attitudes towards women's role in agriculture, and particularly their decisive impact on the provision of basic staple food for their families and society as a whole. In Africa, the notion of women being primarily occupied in subsistence agriculture needs to be corrected as well. "Male and female dynamics, which are culturally specified, play an extremely important role in determining the impact of broader social and economic trends on women and their capacity to respond to such trends", says the Survey.

With the background of all these misperceptions and fallacies, not to speak of statistical errors, it is no wonder that efforts towards agricultural development have not been very successful. Starvation and hunger have remained a constant plague in many developing countries, in spite of "astronomic" advances elsewhere in science and technology and in other economic areas.

The Survey enumerates the ways in which agricultural and rural development programmes have been jeopardized because the actual and potential roles of women were not taken into consideration. In particular:

"(a) Women's work overload was not taken into consideration, and no labour-saving technology was introduced to alleviate this overload;

"(b) Women's performance of particular agricultural tasks was overlooked, and agricultural information and training was not directed to women;

"(c) Women's involvement as independent farmers or livestock-keepers was overlooked, and women were largely left out of integrated rural development and other agricultural programmes;

"(d) An increase in family income was identified with increases in women's income, often to the detriment of women;

"(e) Women's labour was considered as 'family' labour to be used interchangeably in women's or men's fields for men's crops, curtailing economic and other types of incentives for women;

"(f) Women's special needs and constraints as mothers and wives, as small independent farmers and as heads of household, were not considered in their access to credit and other services."

Development efforts in agriculture and their consequences for women have been different in different regions and countries, depending upon their particular circumstances:

"In Latin America and the Caribbean, agricultural modernization has been characterized on one side by the industrialization of agriculture, which has generally been promoted by national and multinational agro-business, and on the other by agrarian reform. Women have not been fully integrated in either. Women have often been pushed into unskilled casual labour or have been marginalized from agriculture altogether by its industrialization.

"The *Asian* rural structure is characterized by land scarcity and increasing landlessness, where agricultural modernization has generally meant the increase in yields brought about by the introduction of high-yield varieties. The effects on women have varied depending on the type of crops, the tasks culturally assigned to women, the changes in size and seasonal distribution of labour, and the characteristics of the household and the status of women within it.

"In *Sub-Saharan Africa* modernization has generally meant the promotion of productivity for cash crops, which are usually 'men's' crops, at the expense of food crops, which are usually 'women's' crops. The effects on women's status and on food production have been momentous. Since it was 'men's' crops which were promoted, women did not participate in agricultural modernization, food production lagged behind and nutritional levels worsened.

"In the *Middle East and North Africa* male migration has been the recent trend of greatest relevance to women in agriculture. Migration has caused poorer rural areas to be depopulated and women have had to take up men's agricultural tasks, significantly increasing their workload."

According to the World Survey it is essential to focus on the costs, rather than on the benefits, of agricultural modernization and agricultural work for women. The important cost is work overload. Needless to say, overwork has negative effects on women's health, retards the schooling of girls, damages the nutritional status of women and their families, and prevents women from participating in any kind of local decision-making.

Governmental strategies in most countries had little or no effect during the UN Decade for Women on the improvement of women's situation in agriculture. Separate ministries or units on women's issues had not proved very useful, but the creation of women's units within ministries of agriculture or rural development had more positive impact.

The story of the co-operatives is also indicative. In all countries women have insisted upon all-women co-operatives. Their experience in the mixed-sex co-operatives in many cases was that women had to do all the work while men decided and enjoyed the resulting income. Such co-operatives only aggravated inequalities, both in income and decision-making. And yet policy-makers and international experts have persistently resisted the establishment of all-women co-operatives, in spite of the fact that, where they have been established, they have proved to be very successful (e.g. in India, Bangladesh, Cameroon, Mali, Lesotho, Ghana, etc.) They have allowed women to plan their own production, control the allocation of their time and labour, and decide the use of income in the way they deem appropriate.

The power relationship between men and women in rural families seems to play an extremely important role. Transition to a monetary economy always enhances the power of men, both in society and in the family. In this process agricultural extension work and Western patterns of thinking have really had a damaging effect upon the position of women in families and rural societies. Money becomes a new symbol of power for men, and thus makes them ever more ready to emphasize cash crop production, even at the expense of the family food supply. The so-called modernization of agriculture has seriously squeezed women's subsistence farming, and has sometimes forced them to abandon food crops altogether. This has a lot to do with failures in the alleviation or solution of food scarcity problems.

Therefore, the Survey emphasizes strongly the empowerment of women by building up their self-confidence and assertiveness. It is a critical part of the strategy to increase productivity of agriculture:

"This process of empowering entails much more than awareness of alternatives, women's rights and the nature of the requirements. It involves the breakdown of powerful sex stereotyping, which prevents women from demanding their rights from men in positions of authority", states the

Survey. "The consequences of patriarchy for agricultural productivity are very expensive; developing countries cannot bear their heavy cost."

The impact of improvements in women's role upon the achievement of overall development goals is explicitly addressed in the Survey:

"Improving women's role in development has the immediate effect of *increasing equality between sexes*. It has also the effect of accelerating the process of *agricultural development*, increasing the level of *national production* and the supply of food at the national and local levels. Simultaneously, it has the effect of making development *more responsive to human needs*."[3] (Emphasis added by authors.)

Money and finance

The issue of money and finance, says the World Survey, has indeed received little attention in discussions concerning women, much less than, for example, those of industry and agriculture, because its relationship to women — and the consequences of processes and policies in this sector on women — are difficult to define. The preparation of the World Survey may have been the very first time, at least within the UN context, that this issue has even been considered.

Nevertheless it is extremely important, since this sector in each society is in fact the real power centre today insofar as the policies and control of economic life and development are concerned. The Survey includes in this sector private banking, financial institutions and public bureaucracies (national and local treasuries and ministries of finance) — the sector responsible for policies on balance of payments, inflation, national monetary and budgetary matters, credits and loans and structural adjustment measures.

It is stated right at the beginning of the Survey that the relation between women's share of employment in this sector and the financial and monetary strategies of institutions operating in it is very weak. This is true irrespective of the proportion of the women's share, which varies from 5% in developing countries to more than half in some developed economies. Everywhere in these institutions women hold the lowest-paid positions without any power of decision, which in this powerful field is almost exclusively in the hands of men. Inequality of power between men and women seems to be extreme in this field.

In this sector it is also more meaningful and interesting to assess the effects on women of international trends in money and finance, and their national responses, than to trace the possible benefits of their participation. The Survey explores the consequences of orthodox monetarist policies intended to control balance of payments instability, worsening terms of trade, and growing debt service on societies in general and on women in particular. These problems have increased since the World Survey was drafted, and have been the major focus of development discussions in the 1980's.

Structural adjustment policies have severe implications for social services and other public spending, for employment and salaries, and in the long run for provision of basic needs. In many countries transfer payments to the private enterprise sector are made at the expense of those most in need, especially women, who share a heavy burden of increased indirect taxation and are likely to be more negatively affected than men by reductions in social expenditure.

Women have an essential impact also upon a country's competitiveness; the comparative advantage of its export production is due to low salaries, no social benefits, and lack of job security for their women labourers. This kind of competitiveness has been called competition at the expense of human (woman's!) sweat and not based on intelligence and organization.

The Survey concludes that, in general, women appear to be more affected than men by macro-economic adjustment forces. Most adjustment policies tend to have a regressive effect on income distribution and employment, to increase poverty and to degrade living conditions. The gap between men and women widens. It is clear that women have shouldered more heavily than men the burden of the deflationary macro-economic adjustment process applied in many of the developing countries.

The Survey also points out that, in those countries where growth has nevertheless taken place, the wide gap between economic opportunities open to men and women has not been reduced in proportion to increases achieved. The gap seems to widen more particularly in the lower socio-economic segments of society.

As measures for improving the situation of women in the fields of money and finance, the Survey recommends that the social effects of all adjustment policies should be kept in mind in all planning and formulation of such policies. At least the sacrifices implicit in adjustment ought to be justly distributed. One might wonder, however, when reading the recommended remedies, whether they represent only wishful thinking or whether possibilities for concrete implementation have been seriously considered.

This part of the Survey emphasizes many of the same aspects dealt with in previous chapters: the importance of improving women's formal education, provision of adult education services, permanent education, professional and on-the-job training, extension services and other social services. Improvement in the productivity of women's work, and policies more oriented towards import substitution, are seen as ways of reducing the need for foreign exchange and increasing national self-reliance. And here again it is pointed out that monetary and fiscal policies more respectful of human resources will not only improve equality between men and women but also make development more sensitive to human needs.

The chapter ends with an interesting hint that women's culture might be a source of ideas and practices for an alternative and altogether more human culture: "The awareness of the enormous potential of women as a human resource for development might then be one of the first steps for an alternative development model."

Science and technology

The World Survey gives a brief indicative picture of that peculiar phenomenon which has taken place within the so-called scientific revolutionary process: on the one hand, rapid economic and technological progress in the industrial-

ized world, and on the other hand increasing inequalities
in general. The disparities between continents and countries
have continued to grow, and ever more rapidly. "Industrial
growth has meant increasing inequality of wealth and
opportunity overall, and greater inequality of employment by
sex", writes Zenebeworke Tadesse, who has prepared a study
for UNITAR on this subject.

The advancement of science and technology affects people
in all walks of life, but tends to affect men and women very
differently, says the Survey. Some technological changes are
specifically detrimental to women or to particular groups of
women. The world of science and technology has been a
male domain for centuries, in the same way as the church
and the military. Until this century women hardly even
had access to universities, where science is taught and technology developed. It is therefore legitimate to say that the
exclusion of women from these fields may be part of the reason why the applications of scientific innovations have been
so slanted, and have brought about increasing inequality.

The Survey discusses the cultural and historical reasons for
women's exclusion, and differences in various cultures and
countries today. It points to an interesting economic phenomenon related to technological progress which has remained largely unrecognised by economists. "As modern
production was separated from the home — one of the pre-
conditions of industrialization — men were separated from
women and children, leaving most of the child care to
women. In addition, women have often been forced to provide cheap labour or even unpaid labour directly to the employer of their husbands."

This — a specific cause of error in economic statistics and
in perceptions of economic growth — is closely linked to the
correlation between economic and social development:

> "Economic activity and progress is traditionally measured
> in terms of purchased goods and services. Thus, by trans-
> ferring any production or service from the unpaid domes-
> tic domain to the market — without changing its amount
> and quality, or even sacrificing some of its quality —
> 'economic growth' is created."

In this sense a significant proportion of statistical economic growth is created just by transferring customary female functions from the 'invisible' family economy to a 'genderless', measurable economy. The invisible thus becomes visible in an economic sense, and also in the national budgetary sense, but at the same time these traditionally female functions have lost much of their significance: women's work is devalued.

The Survey does not, however, seem to perceive that this process is, precisely, a major reason why 'women's work' is paid so little in the labour market, and why women primarily get the jobs which men don't like or are not able to do. And within this process women have also lost a lot of the indigenous power in society which was represented by their specific capabilities and competences.

The Survey is bold enough to refer to the feminist argument that technology in itself has been male-oriented, and to quote Elise Boulding: "The palace-temple-army-technology complex was operated by men, and the kitchen-garden-homecraft-child bearing complex was operated by women." She has also stated that there has been no independent drive in any society to place technology "in the hands of the poor" or "in the hands of women".

If other chapters of the Survey have emphasized the importance of girls' education and full and equal access of women to all levels of schools and universities, the chapter on science and technology puts even greater stress on these aspects. The process needed to 'equalize' the creation and utilization of science and technology could be visualized as a chain reaction (see following page).

In this connection the Survey also emphasizes strongly the importance of political decision-making:

"In particular, the decisions on research for economic and social development would need to be influenced by persons who know about the effects technology has or is likely to have on women. The closer design and development come to the typical everyday experience of women, the more valuable the technology will be to women."

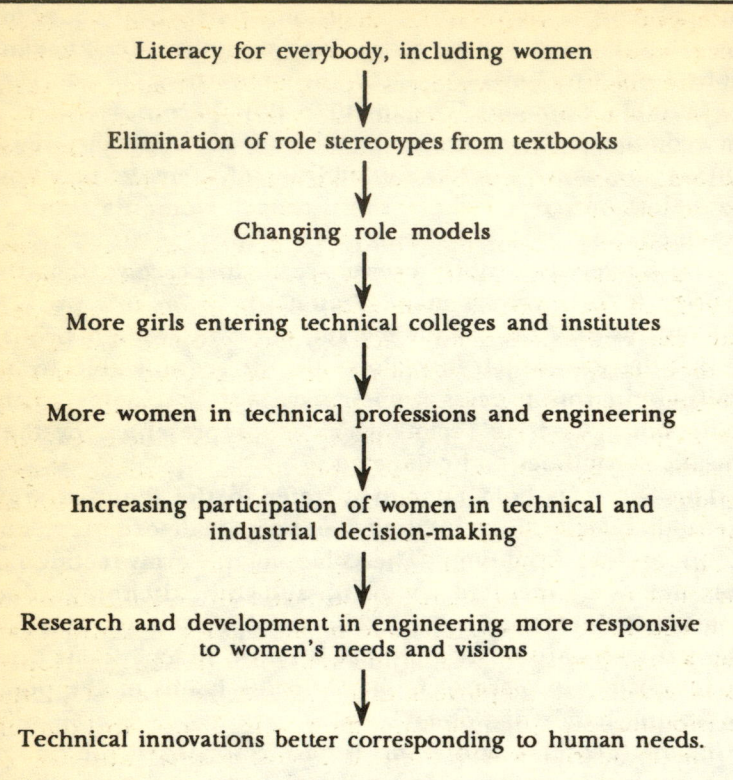

Literacy for everybody, including women

Elimination of role stereotypes from textbooks

Changing role models

More girls entering technical colleges and institutes

More women in technical professions and engineering

Increasing participation of women in technical and
industrial decision-making

Research and development in engineering more responsive
to women's needs and visions

Technical innovations better corresponding to human needs.

The Survey is, however, very realistic in recognizing that "implementation of such recommendations will take a long time unless the share of women at the decision-making (including law-making) levels is significantly increased".

Trade

The Survey focuses primarily on internal trade in developed and developing countries, since the international aspects of trade and their consequences on women have been dealt with in connection with both agriculture and industry. Trade, seen from women's point of view, is indeed a multifaceted issue.

There are major differences distinguishable also between the various categories of countries. In developing countries women's trading is primarily an individual, more or less independent, enterprise for making a livelihood for themselves and their families. In industrialized countries women are the majority of employees in the field of trade; not many are independent entrepreneurs or managers of enterprises. In socialist countries women as traders are practically nonexistent, since private business has not been congruent with the ideology.

In certain parts of the Third World, such as West Africa, the Caribbean and South-East Asia, women handle between 70-90% of the domestic farm and marine produce marketed. The traders themselves are often producers too, and take care of their family responsibilities at the same time. "Generally speaking", says the Survey, "in the developing world trade is the major occupation that allows women to make a living outside the agricultural sector, while in the more developed regions it is just one subdivision of the service sector, with no apparent special significance (for women)."

The Survey also examines why women seem to be so attracted to trade in some regions, and the implications of such activities. Women in trade in developing countries can play a highly visible and influential role. In the developed world women as employees carry little or no weight in the decision-making process, and their role is not influential. In the industrial world there is almost a total absence of women in top business jobs. The only exception is the USA, where just over 10% of managerial positions are held by women.

Generally speaking, according to the Survey, the proportion of economically active female population engaged in trade is small — less than 20% — with the exception of Ghana and Nigeria. It is possible that these rates do not fully reflect the reality, partly because many women are traders only as a part-time activity, and because much of the informal economy is not reflected in official figures.

The heterogeneity of women traders and differences between various groups are also revealed in the Survey. One major group among rural women traders are actually subsistence farmers but often sell some of their surplus as processed foodstuffs. They can also sell handicrafts and other non-food products. Another group consists of more professional women traders who specialize in marketing farm and marine pro-

duce at retail or wholesale levels. In some countries they reg-
ulate the major part of the foodstuff supply to urban areas. The
third major group comprises urban women exclusively in
petty retail or wholesale trade, who sell everything from
food to expensive jewellery.

Within the last two categories there are also some very
wealthy women. Although in the minority, their social impact is tremendous. They have achieved an economic and social status of which they are very proud; they symbolize the
kind of success women can aspire to, and become role models
for other women traders. This is part of the reason why
trade is so popular among women in many developing countries.

Women in trade are very closely linked everwhere with
the so-called informal sector of the economy. The informal
economy, however, seems to be the kind of phenomenon
which escapes exact definition. It consists of both monetary
and non-monetary activities, and is in many cases a manifestation of the inaccuracy of national statistics. According to
existing studies and estimates, "the share of the urban labour
force in Third World cities engaged in the informal sector
range anywhere from 20 to 70 per cent, the average being
close to half or more".

At the present time of economic crisis, especially in Africa
and Latin America, the informal economy and all kinds of
activities therein seem to be a lifeline for the multitude of
people expelled from the formal economy. This is so especially for women who have never had access to it but, in this
crisis situation, have the ever-growing burden of providing
for the livelihood of their families. In some countries the informal economy has, indeed, demonstrated enormous expansion and dynamism in situations where the macro-economy
fails or collapses.

In the industrial world, trade and business structures contain an ever-growing potential for power — typically male,
as in centralized power structures everywhere. But how is it
in Third World countries where women seem to occupy
more independent and central positions in trade? Does it
imply that they also hold relative influence in their
societies? The Survey comes to the conclusion that the answer
is both yes and no.

The first benefit to these women is a sense of real independence; in addition to economic independence they escape the tutelage of men. Of necessity they also develop the strong and independent personality that goes with business. In West Africa the particular independence of women as individuals is well seen also in their relationships with men in marriage and as parents.

There are examples of the influence of these women traders which indicate that some have, indeed, been able to use their economic power to obtain also political power. Nevertheless, few women traders are in important political positions or have access to the spheres of highest political power in their countries. In many cases women, though recognized as powerful, have been unable to influence decisions of political organs which are against their interests. The conclusion of the Survey is that their political influence and power are rather limited. This seems to be contrary to the experience in many countries, where men in significant positions in business life often achieve growing influence in politics as well.

Future trends for women traders are not promising. In spite of a certain independence, trading as a livelihood is very insecure and risky for women in developing countries. Although in some countries the informal activity of women seems to be flourishing for the time being — due to crises in the formal economy — the trend in general seems to be following that in industrialized countries.

The expansion of enterprises, modernization and overall urbanization and monetarization of society is accompanied by the transition of business into male hands. More and more men are taking over trade sectors formerly controlled by women. They have much better access to the money needed to increase investment, and they have that freedom from ties and responsibilities — and thus mobility — that many women do not have. At the same time, business is becoming more and more Westernized, i.e. increasingly aggressive, competitive, and seen as an end in itself. The prospect seems to be that women, also in developing countries, will become only the servants and employees of trade instead of being its owners and decision-makers.

The World Survey's consideration of women and trade omits altogether the other side of the coin, women as buyers and consumers. And yet this is the role which women have everywhere; the majority of purchasing decisions in the commercial sector are made by women. This is increasingly the case also in developing countries as the role of independent traders declines. Through their roles as consumers and clients women could acquire significant power in industrial societies; they could control demand and supply, define taste, and reject consumerist manipulation by developing an awareness conducive to that kind of conscious behaviour as consumers.

Energy

The picture drawn by the World Survey with regard to women and energy indicates that, in reality, women are involved only as long as human energy, and energy derived directly from nature with physical labour, are concerned. All other energy forms, together with development and research, policies and decision-making on them, etc., are in the male domain. Interestingly enough, the Survey includes also *animate energy*, i.e. human energy with draught animal power, which in industrial countries is almost forgotten and is not included in energy statistics. On the other hand, such energy sources as hydro- and wind-power are to a large extent forgotten.

This portrayal of women and energy problems is well-known. In recent decades there has emerged 'the other energy crisis' in a major part of the Third World, where sources of wood have become more and more scarce and the burden upon women of collecting any kind of fuel from nature has constantly increased. And yet they use fuel almost entirely, and only, for cooking, which on the world scale and in proportion to energy consumption in developed countries represents only a minor amount. The contrast in this respect is particularly glaring, in that the rich world constantly increases wasteful energy use for industry, transport, electrical heating and cooling, not to mention status appliances for all kinds of more or less unnecessary purposes, while poor women in developing countries cannot get even the small amount of fuel they need in order to cook meals for their families.

Rural people in many developing countries are driven in an impossibly vicious circle; the more widely and thoroughly they have to cut and collect usable fuel from nature, the more certainly they promote the desertification of their environment. And yet these women simply have no choice.

"The impact of fuel shortages on rural women in developing countries is dramatic", concludes the Survey, which presents many examples of the various problems faced in policies and programmes aiming to solve the situation. One of the most shocking phenomena is the distribution of labour between men and women in many societies, allotting responsibility for domestic fuel supply entirely to women. Women are overburdened by the multitude of their chores, yet men do not share in this labour.

There are even examples of men who have sabotaged the efforts of women to plant and grow wood, obviously because the field of forestry is again considered to be a male preserve. The Survey refers to a case in Tanzania, where "... half the population may have withdrawn its support for woodlot because firewood collection is traditionally women's work". Common sense would question whether the distribution of labour between men and women in those countries is really so sacred that nobody — the government, donors, the United Nations, the women themselves — can intervene. Would it not be only fair that men would take part of the burden from women by collecting or supplying the fuel? Women in the North have not hesitated to demand — or persuade — their men to participate in baby care, which certainly was not a male chore a few decades ago. Government provisions for parental leave, or even for paternity leave, certainly help.

The Survey indicates clearly that the difference between successful and unsuccessful forestry and energy programmes corresponds exactly with the extent of women's integration. "International aid programmes and experimental projects generally bypass women, despite evidence that training women constitutes the critical difference between successful and unsuccessful programmes in village energy projects, notably those aimed at establishing fuel-wood plantations, rejuvenating forests and introducing new cooking technologies."

If women are not adequately integrated in training and implementation at the local level, neither are they integrated — consulted, invited to participate, listened to — in planning and decision-making on energy-related issues at the country level. And where are the women when OPEC and other oil-producing countries are negotiating, or when the International Atomic Energy Agency is working on the so-called peaceful uses of nuclear energy at the international level?

The fact that women in industrial countries have been actively demonstrating and lobbying against nuclear power for several years is a strong indication of their desire to influence and be heard in the energy policies of their countries. "They are concerned, inter alia, about the effects of radiation on their health and the health of future generations, environmental protection, the arms race and the male-dominated nature of this field of scientific development", reports the Survey quite accurately. Nuclear technology — irrespective of whether it is for weapons or energy — and economies and energy policies geared to increasing use of nuclear power are seen by the contemporary women's peace movement as an ultimate manifestation of militarism and patriarchy, and therefore a threat to everything which is significant to women.

In this connection the Survey emphasizes again the importance of education and training of women in energy technology, economics and the environment. Only when women have appropriate knowledge and training will they be able to participate fully in the management of these issues. A major problem for both management and training is, again, the lack of gender-specific information which could reflect the nature of the use, development and conservation of energy by women and men. Energy surveys are generally based on methods found successful in industrial Western countries, where women are not thought to have anything to say with regard to energy and related policies.

The Survey's overall recommendation is that women need to be organized as women if they want their interests and values to be represented in energy use and planning.

Emerging human perspectives

The most important conclusion of the Survey is that development in general will become more humane, and reflect essential human needs better, if the feminine perspective is taken as the guiding principle. Bringing this perspective into development theories and economics, and into planning and policies, will bring development back to its only legitimate aim — the well-being of the human race, neither more nor less. The interests of women are the interests of human beings, of children and of the whole human family, including men.

Although this basic viewpoint is made very clear in the Survey, it does not try to develop any new philosophy or theory of development as such. In some respects it also interprets women's interests all too narrowly, with jobs and opportunities for women still seen only in quantitative rather than qualitative terms. Nevertheless, it makes it very clear that the so-called Western model of development is all too simplistic and narrow; it has steered world development onto a track which is not sustainable in the long run, and is not even servicing the human good in general.

The need for more thorough examination of development thinking, especially from the women's point of view, is emphasized in Part Eight of the Survey. Entitled "The Concept of Self-reliance and the Integration of Women into Development", it has been prepared by INSTRAW, the International Research and Training Institute for the Advancement of Women, and recognizes that "the self-reliance strategy presupposes an integral approach to development, and with regard to the improvement of the position of women it fully respects their multidimensional development role".

But the main precondition for the realization of the self-reliant approach "is the self-identification of the developmental role of women ... The desired role of women in development should be defined largely in the first place by women themselves, both through their more intensive general social and political involvement and through their proper organization." This section calls for re-examination of development models and their adaptation "to the desire of the people to continually change and improve their social and productive positions. This process should start with the evolution of a critical awareness of the need to change the economic and social role of every person." And it is bold enough to say that "it is only by changing the role of women in society that the society itself can be changed".

Another assessment on women and development

Parallel to the World Survey another study on Women's Participation in Development was prepared by the United Nations Development Programme, for presentation to and use by the World Conference in Nairobi in 1985.[4]

This survey is based on country studies in four countries, one from each main development region (Rwanda, Democratic Yemen, Indonesia and Haiti) and is inter-organizational in that it assesses the contributions of the United Nations development system — i.e. all the UN organs and agencies with substantial development activities — to women's participation in development in those countries. At the same time it is also a follow-up to an earlier UNDP evaluation study in the same countries (except one) five years earlier, dealing with rural women's participation in development, which was presented to the Mid-Decade Conference in Copenhagen in 1980.[5]

The present study focuses in depth on the situation in the countries concerned, bringing a concrete country-level perspective to the issues and problems discussed in the World Survey. It is based on field surveys, whereas the World Survey was produced primarily as desk work based on existing studies and research from various sources. As a follow-up study it also tries to assess and register to what extent the recommendations and plans made on the basis of the first study had been implemented and were influencing the situation of women in those countries. As an inter-organizational study it looks at the work of various organs of the UN System in a comprehensive way, assessing also to what extent they work in a coherent fashion at the country level. Altogether, it shows to what extent the aims of the United Nations Decade for Women were taken seriously at the practical level by both UN agencies and member governments in the sample countries.

Activities performed by women are divided into three categories: production of goods and services, so-called reproduction and maintenance of the human capital, and social functions. The third category consists of activities performed as part of traditional customs or political processes, including many duties and obligations which women are often supposed to perform, irrespective of whether they involve an economic dimension or not. It is often necessary to work in this area in order to get a project accepted and implemented. The study makes an effort to recognize such factors as community and familial norms, as well as religious beliefs which are not always taken into account but may appear to be decisive determinants for the success of projects. It is also well aware that efforts which focus solely on women easily overlook the responsibility of men and inadvertently promote and reinforce existing sex roles.

It is not surprising that the findings of this study confirm the conclusions of several other assessments, for example the World Survey. In the course of the UNDW recognition of the importance of women's participation in development has also increased at government level. Nevertheless, there continues to be a lack of understanding of women's role in society and in development planning, and thus a loss of development potential. Women are still often seen only as consumers of social services, and not as producers of goods, services and welfare.

Compared with men, women lack access to resources, services and facilities; they are under-educated and overworked. In many instances these conditions have reached the point at which they are slowing down the development process, says the study. Often women's activities continue to be viewed only within the context of a gesture towards equity; they are not incorporated into mainstream development, in spite of the fact that women play a crucial role in most economic and social sectors. In practice, less than one in every six projects deemed to affect women's lives and work were designed to involve women in project activities.

The findings and recommendations of the UNDP study are, in principle, addressed to the UNDP itself and the UN development system, as well as to member governments. In order to fulfill its mandate, says the study, the UN development system should above all take full cognizance of women as a development resource in need of the same attention as the male half of the population. There are policy guidelines and instructions to this effect, but more often than not they are neglected or simply not known. They should be seen as an obligation, to be applied with vigour and consistency.

Among its recommendations the study emphasizes three main categories of measures for improvement:

— As a matter of strategy, women's role in development, as participants and beneficiaries, should be an issue of substance in all key programming events for technical cooperation, such as preparations of country programmes, Donors' Round Tables and the identification and design of projects and programmes. Women should be included at least in the last category of events to ensure that participation is not confined to men's ideas of appropriate roles.

— An adequate database should be developed, since without reliable information sensible planning is not possible. Information should cover such issues as division of labour between men and women, women's access to and control of resources, traditional systems of social organization, etc. Baseline surveys should be undertaken and complementary information collected. Mechanisms for monitoring and evaluation of programmes from women's point of view need to be established.

— Substantive staff training on women and development issues is urgently needed at all levels of government and United Nations staff.

In conclusion, the UNDP study finds it important and realistic to note that "plans and programmes of action that have emerged from the UN Decade for Women cover a vast area and require substantive and substantial changes in firmly entrenched attitudes and behaviour. Consequently, it is not realistic to expect profound changes to occur overnight. Viewed from this perspective, the progress that has been made by Governments and UN organizations is substantial."

This statement was made in 1985. The UNDP study has, *inter alia*, been part of the groundwork on which a constant effort to integrate women and development issues has been based; it is a substantial part of the work that UNDP is coordinating and conducting as a central organ of the UN development system. We shall discuss further steps within this process in later pages.

The voice of women themselves

The voice of the North — even though not necessarily of Northern women — is often heard loudly in the development debate at world fora. The voice from the South needs to be articulated and heard more than in the past. At the Nairobi *Forum '85* a group of Southern women presented a very pertinent intervention.

> "Economic development, that magic formula, devised sincerely to move poor nations out of poverty, has become women's worst enemy. Roads bring machine-made ersatz goods, take away young girls and food and traditional art and culture; technologies replace women, leaving families even further impoverished. Manufacturing cuts into natural resources (especially trees), pushing fuel and fodder sources further away, bringing home-destroying floods or life-destroying drought, and adding all the time to women's work burdens."

This is how Devaki Jain from India, the initiator and first convener of the DAWN group, assessed development in recent decades in a 1984 essay.[6] DAWN (Development Alternatives with Women for a New Era) is a group of 22 Third World women researchers and activists, representing all three main development continents, who first came together in Bangalore, India, in August 1984 and decided to prepare an independent report on world development for the Nairobi Conference from a Third World women's perspective.

In the short time available before the Conference they were able to produce a strong and factual report: *Development, Crises and Alternative Visions: Third World Women's Perspective,* which made a considerable impact at Forum '85 and has since been one of the basic documents on development.[7] At the beginning of their report they declare that:

> "We are now more aware of the need to question in a more fundamental way the underlying processes of devel-

opment into which we have been attempting to integrate women. Throughout the Decade it has been implicit that women's main problem in the Third World has been insufficient participation in an otherwise benevolent process of growth and development. Increasing women's participation and improving their shares in resources, land, employment and income relative to men were seen as both necessary and sufficient to effect dramatic changes in their economic and social position. Our experiences now lead us to challenge this belief."

The group draws not only on the experiences and findings of the UN Decade for Women but on the history of the past, reaching far back to the times of colonialism and its heritage. They assess and evaluate the whole process of social development, both theoretically and practically, and claim that "many of the issues raised — including the very meaning of development itself — are equally relevant to the more industrialized countries". This argument is in fact confirmed by the World Survey itself, in which many parallels are drawn between developing and developed countries, pointing out commonalities in the outcome and consequences of development on women both North and South.

DAWN dissociates itself from traditional equality-oriented development thinking, as it has been implemented mechanically and statistically. "Equality for women is impossible within the existing economic, political and cultural processes that reserve resources, power and control for small sections of people. But neither is development possible without greater equity for and participation by women."

DAWN's point of departure is feminism which, according to their definition, is a political movement and "has at its very core a process of economic and social development geared to human needs through wider access to economic and political power. Equality, peace and development by and for the poor and oppressed are inextricably interlinked with equality, peace and development by and for women." The link between the poor and women informs the whole reasoning of DAWN-Report. As a matter of fact the majority of women in the world are poor, and the majority of the poor in the world are women.

The UN's World Survey and DAWN's report were prepared in parallel but independently. They naturally have a lot of the same data and research, and are very different in style of presentation, but in a significant way they complement and confirm each other's findings and conclusions.

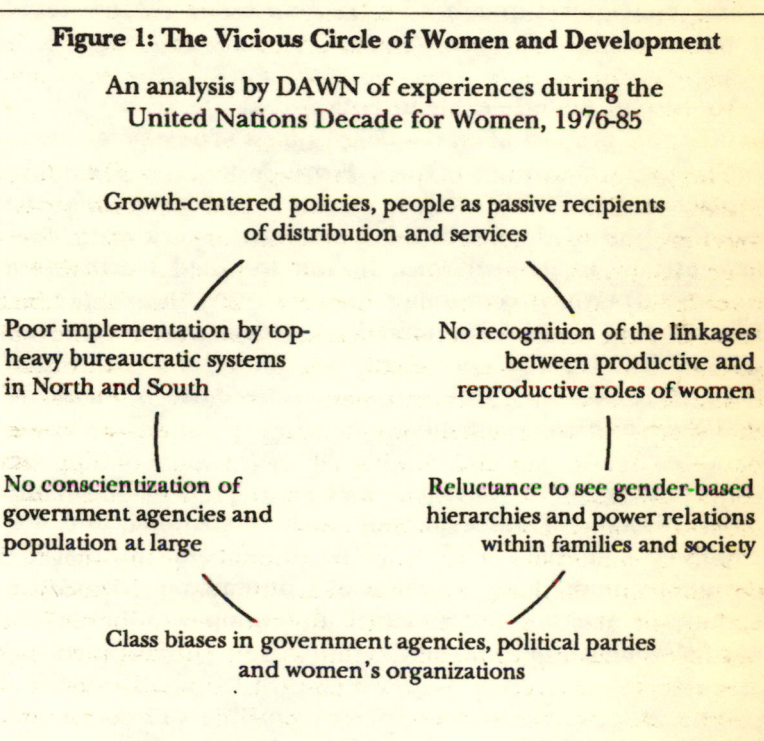

Figure 1: The Vicious Circle of Women and Development

An analysis by DAWN of experiences during the United Nations Decade for Women, 1976-85

Growth-centered policies, people as passive recipients of distribution and services

Poor implementation by top-heavy bureaucratic systems in North and South

No recognition of the linkages between productive and reproductive roles of women

No conscientization of government agencies and population at large

Reluctance to see gender-based hierarchies and power relations within families and society

Class biases in government agencies, political parties and women's organizations

Source: This chart is based on a background paper for *DAWN-Report* prepared by the meeting in Bangalore, August 1984 (Gita Sen).

The DAWN report speaks out in a very straightforward manner, without any political reservations or considerations, and goes even further: It is not satisfied only to analyze and describe, it proposes visions for the future and about the future as they, women, wish to see it. The third and last chapter in the report is devoted to alternative visions, strategies and methods.

"First, our consciousness and ethics now need to be crystallized into a clear vision of what we want society to be like and what we want for women. Second, we need strategies that will get us from here to there, take us beyond the small and fragmented efforts of the Decade ... Third, we want to spell out the methods for actualizing our visions and strategies through the empowerment of individual women and their organizations."

The group underlines its intention that the report will be just the first product of an ongoing process. The emergence of this prominent group of Third World women is a decisive step forward, not only in their emancipation but also in the emancipation of the South in its ability to speak ever more authentically in its own voice in the so-called North-South dialogue. DAWN is continuing its work, with the support of thousands of women and men both North and South, and has acquired a status comparable to *Third World Forum* and other male authority groups. Its voice needs to be heard in both the North and the South:

"... what we have learned is our most precious asset: the rich diversity of our experiences, understanding, and ideologies combined with a growing recognition that we cannot propose a social/political/economic programme for women alone, but that we need to develop one for society, from women's perspectives."

Five years later...

Since the first *World Survey on the Role of Women in Development* was found to be an invaluable asset for the Nairobi Conference it was logical that, in endorsing the *Forward-looking Strategies 1985,* the UN General Assembly should also decide that the Secretary-General should update the World Survey on a regular basis. It was requested that the first regular update be presented to the General Assembly five years after the first, i.e. in 1989. This was a very important decision, implying that from now on development would be reviewed from women's point of view as well, and not only from the economic or 'general' point of view.

The original World Survey recorded and emphasized the important role played by women in the world economy. The first regular update[8] centres on more complex questions; how women play their role, the factors that enhance or impede them, and the kind of issues that must be addressed if women's full and equal participation in the economy is to be achieved. The approach is more analytical than descriptive, due to a dramatic increase in research on the economic role of women.

The story told by the 1989 Survey is illuminating but not at all encouraging about progress and trends since 1984. We can just take up some of the main lines of the assessment:

"The 1980's have seen one of the longest periods of growth ever recorded; but for developing countries, especially in Africa and Latin America, it has meant that development has virtually stopped.

"Development has not been occurring. This is particularly true for women ... while some have improved their position, far more have become poor. Ironically, poverty among women has increased, even within the richest countries, resulting in a 'feminization of poverty'". Poverty particularly afflicted families in which women are the sole income earners, a growing phenomenon.

"... Women entered the labour force in large numbers, saw improvements in access to education in most regions, began to appear in sectors where they were previously absent, made up a slightly larger proportion of managerial and technical jobs. But ... the rate of improvement in all of these indicators was slower than in the previous decade.

"... increases in maternal and infant mortality in some developing countries have been observed for the first time in decades as social services have been cut as part of adjustment packages.

"The bottom line shows that ... despite economic progress in some developing countries, economic progress for women has virtually stopped, social progress has slowed, social well-being in many cases has deteriorated...

"Women, however, remain a major force for change ... Development for women means development for society."

It is obvious that the five years since 1984 have been a period of uneven growth that has aggravated the differences between the regions, and particularly between North and South. In the older industrial countries the long period of steady economic growth has meant an unprecedented increase in material consumption. In most developing regions, however, stagnation or regression of the economy have led to a deterioration in the situation of women as individuals, and as carers and providers of families and households. Pre-existing conditions of inequality between men and women — in health and nutrition, in levels of literacy and training, in access to education and economic opportunity and participation in decision-making at all levels — have sometimes been exacerbated both by the crises themselves and by the policies adopted to cope with them.

Development in the 1980's has not followed the lines prescribed in the International Development Strategy for this third UN Development Decade. The question is whether this is the failure of the Strategy or of its implementation? "However, there is no automatic link between economic growth and the advancement of women, even in a limited material sense", says the 1989 Survey. "One major shortcoming of development strategies has been the failure to take into account the role and potential of women. The facts suggest that this shortcoming must be remedied if the development strategies of the 1990's are to succeed."

The 1989 Survey focuses particularly on the effects on women of *external debt and adjustment policies*. It contains an extensive review of the effects of adjustment policies on women's income development, employment, education, maternal and child mortality, malnutrition and social situation. It recognizes the same trends which were already seen in the first Survey, and makes a more thorough study of the situation in the latter part of the 1980's. The general impact of adjustment in many countries affects progress towards improving the status of women, which has often stagnated, with pre-existing conditions of inequality becoming even worse. Positive developments in the fields of maternal and infant mortality have come to a halt in many countries, and death rates have begun to increase again after many decades of steady decline.

The worldwide increase in *female-headed households* has been particularly pronounced during this period. Many social and cultural factors have contributed to this, but responses to more difficult economic conditions, male migration, female participation in the workforce and family breakdown have accelerated the process. Female-headed households tend to be among the poorest in all countries for which data is available, and this has grave implications for the present well-being and future advancement of women and their dependents.

The 1989 Survey has a very comprehensive and substantive chapter on the *crucial importance of women to food and agricultural production*, which also gives due recognition to the importance of environmental factors to women — a factor which has been inadequately discussed in earlier reviews and surveys. The situation in many countries reflects the fact that rural women suffer the major burden of environmental distress; they work ever longer hours to produce enough food and income for their families and to collect fuel and water, with less family labour due to male migration.

It is also made clear that, contrary to common assumptions, the collection of firewood in rural areas is not the major cause of deforestation. "The main causes are large-scale lumbering, agricultural expansion, overuse of agricultural land, burning forests to encourage fodder growth, and overgrazing."

Then the 1989 Survey gives new assessments on trends in *industrialization,* the *service sector* and the *informal sector,* as well as in all forms of paid work. There are also substantive reviews on women's preparation for and participation in all aspects of technological change, as well as on UN work for the development of statistics and indicators to better reflect all aspects of women's contributions to the well-being of their families and societies as a whole.

Two new aspects are also raised; one chapter discusses the *role of culture* in the advancement of women, while another studies the *interrelationships between equality, development and peace,* as premised in the Forward-looking Strategies of Nairobi. These are important new aspects in the work for the advancement of women. We know that sex roles and societal attitudes on the status of men and women are culturally based. On the other hand, the cultural heritage carries the values and traditions which are the universally irreplaceable substance of human existence and identity. These must be studied by each generation in recognition of their lasting importance and the need to rectify and reinterpret them in the light of equality, justice and peace.

To sum up, the 1989 Survey turns to the economic crisis as the main phenomenon affecting women's lives now and in recent years. Closer analysis shows, however, that the effects of the economic crisis are "not always those that might be naively expected, nor are they always negative ... What is clear is that, although often unnoticed, women affect and are affected by international and national policies in ways that are only beginning to be understood, and that merit further examination. Indeed, *examining economic conditions through a 'gender lens' is an effective way of incorporating the human dimension into economic planning and policy-making.*" (Emphasis added by the authors.)

As emerging issues of particular relevance for future analyses the new Survey mentions three: women's participation in economic decision-making, the relationship between women's economic role and the support functions provided within the family, and women's involvement in the crucial issue of the environment. These issues should be given increased attention in the forthcoming second regular update of the World Survey, which is to appear in 1994.

The second updated Survey will also take up the question of the relationship of international economic policies — international trade, its terms and policies, export orientation in developing countries, the policies of international finance and monetary institutions, etc. — to women's situation and economic role. It is also proposed to devote more attention to the examination of the family and household as the basic economic unit in society, and to women's roles as managers within it, and to strengthen the emphasis given to the human dimension — the family in the development process, poverty, income distribution, quality of life, social support measures and violence against women, both within the family and in society.

Comparing the Survey and its first update, one can say that the former assessed development from women's point of view much more than just for one decade. Therefore it presented a lot of new, even dramatic information. The 1989 Survey is not necessarily as exciting a new spotlight upon the life of the world's women, but it brings more depth to the issues. If the first Survey had a message — that to a large extent development has not benefitted women — the new one has an even less positive message; since, during the period it covers, the situation in most developing countries has only deteriorated, it is little wonder that women have suffered.

But women have also proved to be a lifeline for others, particularly in difficult times. Because of the opportunities and possibilities found in particular in the informal sector, and their inherent skills and toughness, women have been able to relieve the worst of the hardships. Nevertheless, they have paid a high price, as increasing mortality figures for mothers and infants indicate.

The most important thing is that the situation be monitored from the women's point of view. Now the international community has an instrument for following up the situation, and the sources and mechanisms for obtaining information are constantly improving. This is the prerequisite for influencing matters in a realistic manner, and for proposing policies and programmes for the future.

It is also important that governments decide now on the provision of adequate resources for the UN Division for the Advancement of Women, to enable Survey updates to be prepared on a regular basis. Consolidation of the mechanism for producing regular updates would also confirm the status of the World Survey on the Role of Women in Development as an important and respected working asset for the whole UN System, as has been the case with the World Economic Survey and the World Social Survey over a number of decades.

Both the World Survey and its first update are irreplaceable sources of information on women and development, so comprehensive that this book can touch upon only a few of the important areas they cover. Those who wish to study these issues or to influence policies concerning them should obtain the actual UN documents and explore them thoroughly. They are of great assistance in bringing the process forward, both in the UN System itself and in national governmental bodies, and will help women's organizations in their efforts to influence and monitor what is going on with regard to women.

Notes

[1] *World Survey on the Role of Women in Development,* United Nations, New York, 1986. A/CONF.116.4/Rev.1, Sales No. E.8.IV.3.

[2] See list of acronyms and addresses.

[3] Doc.A/39/566, paragraph 49.

[4] *Women's Participation in Development: An inter-organizational assessment.* Evaluation Study No. 13, United Nations Development Programme, New York, 1985.

[5] *Rural Women's Participation in Development.* Evaluation Study No. 3, UNDP 1980.

[6] Devaki Jain, "India : A Condition Across Caste and Class", Robin Morgan, (ed.), *Sisterhood is Global.* The International Women's Movement Anthology, Anchor Press/Doubleday, 1984.

[7] Gita Sen and Karen Grown, *Development Crises and Alternative Visions : Third World Women's Perspective,* Monthly Review Press, New York, 1987. (First commercial printing in Norway, 1985).

[8] *1989 World Survey on the Role of Women in Development.* Sales No. E.89.IV.2. Available from Sales Section, Room DC2-853, United Nations, New York.

3.
Forward-looking Strategies
for the Advancement of Women:
Equality — Development — Peace

The final document of the Nairobi Conference, the Forward-looking Strategies for the Advancement of Women,[1] was adopted unanimously after long and strenuous negotiations in the various Commissions of the Conference. This unanimity was a great achievement, and makes implementation of the document in their own countries a much stronger obligation upon all the governments present at the Conference.[2]

It is also an indication of the success of the Nairobi Conference. The Conferences in Mexico City and Copenhagen were not able to reach consensus in their deliberations so as to adopt the final documents unanimously. Maybe this unanimity is a sign of the growing common understanding among women of different countries as a result of the Decade — even among those acting as official delegates.

Substantially, the FLS document is based upon the declarations and plans of action adopted in earlier World Conferences of the UNDW,[3] the International Development Strategy for the Third Development Decade, and the Convention on the Elimination of All Forms of Discrimination against Women, as well as upon negotiations for the establishment of a New International Economic Order.

Its aim is to express women's views on world affairs. And since all human affairs are also women's affairs, the FLS cover everything human under the sky — issues of peace and war, development, human rights, natural resources and environment, culture, politics and economics, relationships between men and women, family and children — everything!

It is an ambitious document of almost 100 pages of cramped UN language, in some 400 paragraphs.

The overall objectives of the Strategies are the same as those of the whole Decade: Equality, Development and Peace. These three objectives are internally interrelated and mutually reinforcing, so that the advancement of one contributes to the advancement of the others. This is emphasized throughout the document.

The definition of the concepts

The introductory chapter of the FLS presents the historical and substantive background of the document, giving a comprehensive assessment of current trends and perspectives concerning the advancement of women towards the year 2000. It also makes clear the basic concepts and how they are defined for the purposes of the document:

"*Equality* is both a goal and a means whereby individuals are accorded equal treatment under the law and equal opportunities to enjoy their rights and to develop their potential talents and skills so that they can participate in national political, economic, social and cultural development, both as beneficiaries and as active agents. For women in particular, equality means the realization of rights that have been denied as a result of cultural, institutional, behavioural and attitudinal discrimination (paragraph 11).

"*Development* means total development, including development in the political, economic, social, cultural and other dimensions of human life as well as the development of the economic and other material resources and the physical, moral, intellectual and cultural growth of human beings. Development also requires a moral dimension to ensure that it is just and responsive to the needs and rights of the individual and that science and technology are applied within a social and economic framework that ensures environmental safety for all life forms on our planet (paragraph 12).

"*Peace* includes not only the absence of war, violence and hostilities at the national and international levels but also the enjoyment of economic and social justice, equality and the entire range of human rights and fundamental freedoms within society" (paragraph 13).

The FLS also define women in a new way compared with all previous UN documents. "The attainment of the goals and objectives of the Decade requires a sharing of this responsibility by men and women and by society as a whole, and requires that women play a central role as intellectuals, policy-makers, decision-makers, planners, and contributors and beneficiaries of development" (paragraph 15).

This is a decisive new step in the recognition of women in the UN vocabulary, as subjects rather than objects in the eyes of the decision-makers of the UN System. If this formula is taken literally, women should no longer be seen as mere labour or human resources, to be integrated more efficiently into the process of development, but as independent, self-aware persons defining their goals and aspirations themselves, and as equal partners whenever their society and development are being designed, planned and decided upon.

This is well clarified in paragraph 16, which explains what "a women's perspective" means:

"The need for women's perspective on human development is critical, since it is in the interest of human enrichment and progress to introduce and weave into the social fabric women's concept of equality, their choices between alternative development strategies and their approach to peace, in accordance with their aspirations, interests and talents. These things are not only desirable in themselves but are also essential for the attainment of the goals and objectives of the Decade."

In this general part of the FLS it is recognized that the results of the UNDW are modest, as indeed the World Survey has indicated. In spectacular contrast to the well-defined goal in paragraph 16 is the picture of reality presented in paragraph 18, which states that "the devaluation of women's productive and reproductive roles, as a result of which the status of women continued to be regarded as secondary to that of men, and the lower priority assigned to promoting the participation of women in development, are historical factors" that limit women in assuming the role to which they are entitled in this document. "Regardless of gains, the structural constraints imposed by a socio-economic framework in which women are second-class persons still limit progress."

A profound change is now needed in the policies and attitudes in each country if real progress is to be made:

"What is now needed is the political will to promote development in such a way that the strategy for the advancement of women seeks first and foremost to alter the current unequal conditions and structures that continue to define women as secondary persons and give women's issues a low priority. Development should now move to another plane in which women's pivotal role in society is recognized and given its true value. That will allow women to assume their legitimate and core positions in the strategies for effecting the changes necessary to promote and sustain development" (paragraph 21).

The problems of the natural environment receive little attention in the FLS. In paragraph 28, however, the important role of women "as intermediaries between the natural environment and society", especially with respect to agro-ecosystems, safe water and fuel supplies, as well as, naturally, population growth, is recognized. Women should be able to exercise their right to family planning and "an improvement in the situation of women could bring about a reduction in mortality and morbidity as well as better regulation of fertility and hence of population growth, which would be beneficial for the environment and, ultimately, for women, children and men".

A very realistic conclusion on the consequences of political tensions to the aims of the FLS appears in paragraph 31: "If widespread international tensions continue ... then the attention of policy-makers will be diverted from tasks directly and indirectly relevant to the advancement of women and men, and vast resources will be further applied to military and related activities."

In paragraph 32 there is — somewhat surprisingly — a specific "right to dissent publicly and peacefully from their Government's policies, and to mobilize to increase their participation in the promotion of peace within and between the nations". It would be interesting to know the background to this statement, and the discussions behind it. It could be interpreted to limit rather than liberate women to exercise their full political rights in their societies, especially since a draft formula was rejected in the form: "It will be necessary for women to mobilize and dissociate themselves from all forms of violence, oppression and warfare." This formula would have given women the right, for example, to refuse any military training or militarization of their lives in any form.

The central idea of solidarity among women is somewhat hidden in paragraph 33 where it is stated that, in all efforts to alleviate the obstacles, "success will depend in large measure upon whether or not women can unite to help each other to change their poor material circumstances and secondary status, and to obtain the time, energy and experience required to participate in political life". In this connection also the importance of networking among women is underlined, because it "will increase the effectiveness of the political action taken by women".

The objectives adopted already in Mexico and Copenhagen constitute the basis for the strategies and concrete measures to be pursued up to the year 2000; the obstacles are to be met through concerted global, regional and national efforts. The purpose of the Strategies is to further define the goals and sharpen the measures to tackle those obstacles during the following 15 years.

By the year 2000 at least the following objectives should be achieved:

— Illiteracy should be eliminated (paragraph 35).

— Life expectancy for all women should be at least 65 years, of good quality of life (paragraph 35).

— Every woman should have an opportunity for self-supporting employment (paragraph 35).

— Laws guaranteeing equality for women in all spheres of life must by then be fully and comprehensively implemented to ensure a truly equitable socio-economic framework in which real development can take place (paragraph 35).

— A comprehensive and sustained public campaign should be launched by all governments, in close collaboration with non-governmental organizations, women's groups and research institutions as well as the media and educational institutions, to challenge and abolish all discriminatory perceptions, attitudes and practices by the year 2000 (paragraph 77).

— All governments should have adequate, comprehensive and coherent national women's policies to abolish all obstacles to the full and equal participation of women in all spheres of society (paragraph 78).

— UN Agencies which do not have specific guidelines relating to women in development interlinked with the other aims of the period up to the year 2000 should ensure that they are developed (paragraph 324).

— UN regional commissions should undertake further research on the status of women in their regions up to the year 2000, by developing the necessary database and indicators and by drawing upon inputs from all levels of societies, including perspectives on and by women at the grassroots level (paragraph 352).

— The UN should hold at least one World Conference on Women during the period between 1985 and the year 2000.

These are just a few points selected from the vast document of the Forward-looking Strategies. The whole document, as such, comprises the programme for achieving the goals set forth for the UN Decade for Women 1976-1985. Since the goals were not achieved within the Decade they are now to be achieved at the latest by the year 2000. One can say, perhaps, that the UN Decade for Women has become in fact a quarter of a century.

The FLS makes a special appeal to men and women in the industrialized world:

"Although addressed primarily to Governments, international and regional organizations, and non-governmental organizations, an appeal is made to all women and men in a spirit of solidarity. In particular, it is addressed to those women and men who now enjoy certain improvements in their material circumstances and who have achieved positions where they may influence policy-making, development priorities and public opinion to change the current inferior and exploited condition of the majority of women in order to serve the goals of equality for all women, their full participation in development, and the achievement and strengthening of peace" (paragraph 42).

The FLS document is divided into three main chapters according to the central issues of equality, development and peace. In addition there is one chapter devoted to areas of special concern such as urban poor women, elderly and young women, abused and destitute women, victims of prostitution, women as sole supporters of families, migrant women, indigenous women, etc. The fifth chapter deals with international and regional cooperation. Each chapter studies the obstacles to achievement of adopted goals, then presents the basic strategies and discusses measures for their implementation at the national level.

Equality

One of the main aims of the Decade was the full observance of the equal rights of women and the elimination of *de jure* and *de facto* discrimination. The United Nations System, particularly the Commission on the Status of Women, has worked for four decades to establish standards and to propose measures to prevent discrimination on the grounds of sex. Nevertheless, *de facto* discrimination has not only continued but has even increased in many countries, both developed and developing.

The chapter on equality actually elaborates the issues and the aspects of equality already stipulated in the *Convention on the Elimination of All Forms of Discrimination against Women* (Annex 1). Within less than 10 years almost 100 countries have signed and ratified the Convention. "Legislative enactment is only one element in the struggle for equality", states the FLS, but an important one because "it provides the legitimate basis for action and acts as a catalyst for societal change".

The limitations of legal measures have been experienced in many countries where international conventions on equality and, recently, on the Elimination of All Forms of Discrimination against Women, have been ratified but where discrimination *de facto* still persists, in spite of rectification of the laws and establishment of governmental institutions to monitor their enactment. This is one indication of the deeply-rooted nature of discrimination in the beliefs, traditions, customs and attitudes of many cultures, factors which are more difficult to change than laws.

However, this does not mean that legislation and international conventions are not important. They give invaluable leverage to the demands of citizens and groups who are working actively for equality and justice. But in order to penetrate the subconscious and often mythic roots of sexual discrimination we need also the unprejudiced revelations of feminist research.

The FLS document refers to such factors only in a subtle way when speaking about "a deeply-rooted resistance on the part of conservative elements in society to the change in attitude necessary for a total ban on discriminatory practices against women at the family, local, national and international levels".

A basic strategy for promotion of equality, according to the FLS, is true equality in the sharing of power with men, especially in legislative bodies. But education is given at least the second place among the strategies, meaning both the educational opportunities "to enable women to develop their talents and capabilities for their own personal fulfilment and the benefit of society", and education as a means of eliminating stereotypes and discriminatory and restrictive perceptions of — and attitudes towards — women. This should also apply to the preconceived and stereotypical perceptions of men and the traditional male role in society and culture.

Measures for implementation of the basic strategies at the national level are discussed in three categories: constitutional and legal, social and economic participation, and political participation and decision-making. There is a multitude of issues discussed in over thirty paragraphs, and it is possible here to highlight only a few of them.

Most of the ordinary provisions for equality, such as equality before the law, educational opportunities and training, health services, equality in conditions and opportunities of employment, including remuneration and adequate social security, etc. are naturally listed in the paragraphs of the FLS.

A pertinent point in the light of findings, for example those of the World Survey on the Role of Women in Development, is stipulated in paragraph 62 with regard to agrarian reforms: "Such reforms should guarantee women's constitutional and legal rights in terms of access to land and other means of production, and should ensure that women will control the products of their labour and their income, as well as benefits from agricultural inputs, research, training, credits and other infrastructural facilities."

Another constantly topical problem concerning employment legislation is taken up in paragraph 67. Ordinary employment legislation — often formulated according to Western models — provides security and benefits only for workers employed by somebody, i.e. actual wage earners, but not for those who employ themselves or make important contributions to society in other forms. Therefore, "similar guarantees and benefits should also be extended to women in food production and processing, fisheries and food distribution through trade ... to women working in family enterprises and to other self-employed women, in an effort to give due recognition to the vital contribution of all these informal and invisible economic activities to the development of human resources".

This section also contains many recommendations in the field of family law, on family rights and duties, on ownership of property and in connection with marriage and divorce etc. There are also provisions with regard to appropriate training of judiciary and paralegal personnel concerning the importance of women's rights as set out in international instruments and conventions.

Sometimes these provisions have strange formulations, as in paragraph 76: "Special attention should be given in criminology training to the particular situation of women as victims of violent crimes, including crimes that violate women's bodies and result in serious physical and psychological damage. Legislation should be passed ... to end the degradation of women through sex-related crimes." In its widest sense, this paragraph should provide an umbrella for legislation which should be enacted with regard to violence against women.

This is the only FLS paragraph related to criminology, but even this speaks primarily about "criminology training". The actual legislation on "sex-related crimes" is mentioned only in passing. This paragraph could also be taken to relate to such issues as rape within marriage and other traditional forms of violence again women which still persist in some cases, like sati, burning of young wives, sexual mutilation etc. These are also mentioned as various forms of violence against women in the chapter on Peace (paragraphs 245 and 258).

It is also interesting to note that so-called positive discrimination is included in the FLS as a means of redressing the missing equality between men and women. "Special measures designed to redress the imbalance imposed by centuries of discrimination against women should be promoted to accelerate *de facto* equality between men and women. Those measures should not be considered discriminatory or entail the maintenance of unequal or separate standards. They are to be discontinued when the objectives of equity ... have been achieved."

Development

Just as the chapter on Equality can be seen as parallel to the Convention on the Elimination of All Forms of Discrimination against Women, so the chapter on Development can be seen as parallel to the World Survey on the Role of Women in Development. In principle the FLS chapter on Development should directly reflect the findings of the World Survey; it should outline strategies to redress the failures of the past and to redirect the process of development in ways which will bring about development favourable to women and corresponding to their values and aspirations.

The work of the UN System is, unfortunately, not so consistent. The World Survey was not finalized early enough to be taken in its entirety as the basis for drafting the Forward-looking Strategies. However, there were probably some possibilities for cooperation between the two teams, one drafting the final version of the World Survey and the other working on the draft of the FLS.

The first part of this chapter discusses the obstacles to development appropriate for women. In the beginning, however, it repeats quite a lot of the same arguments used in debates in other fora of the UN System in previous years, not specifically having any women's view at all. It blames "certain developed countries" for preventing the establishment of the New International Economic Order, and emphasizes the seriousness of the aggravating debt crisis and its consequences for women. In fact, all these arguments are true.

At the same time it recognizes the difficulty in harmonizing the objectives of the IDS and the UNDW. One may ask whether this kind of harmonization was seriously attempted, and how it could be done, since neither programme was sufficiently implemented in intergovernmental cooperation? It is hypothetical whether the NIEO, if implemented, would benefit women; the comparative assessment is still to be made between the principles and goals of the NIEO and the FLS.

Critical voices, so clear in both the World Survey and, for example, DAWN-Report, are very subdued in the FLS. The difficulty of altering the sex roles, and thus the increase in women's workload, is recognized, but at least "the exploitative conditions under which women often work have become more visible" during the UNDW.

Developing countries seem to have had difficulty in agreeing that "the historical root causes of women's unequal status are similar" in both North and South. In paragraph 105 it is, however, indirectly admitted that women and men may have different views and priorities in development after all. "Exclusion of women from policy-making and decision-making made it difficult for women ... to include in their preferences and interests the largely male-dominated choices of progress and development." Here it is stated once again that "the issue of women in development has often been perceived as a welfare problem, viewed simply as a cost to the society rather than as a contribution", and therefore of low priority.

Doubts about economic growth as an automatic motor for the advancement of women are expressed also in the FLS. "An evaluation of the experience of the Decade has shed considerable doubt on this over-simplified premise. Consequently, the need to understand better the relationship between development and the advancement of women ... has become greater" (paragraph 103). This is as far as criticism of prevailing development patterns and their consequences goes in the FLS.

When it comes to basic strategies to change the situation, the most important thing is "to remove obstacles to the effective participation of all women in development as intellectuals, policy-makers and decision-makers, planners, contributors and beneficiaries". The commitment to remove these obstacles "should guide the formulation and implementation of policies, plans, programmes and projects, with the awareness that development prospects will be improved and society advanced through the full and effective participation of women".

It is obvious that removal of obstacles to women's participation is basic, but much more is needed. Another basic is the new analysis of development which is being made, especially by DAWN. After women have made their own analysis of past and present development, their full participation in all aspects of development will start to make a real change.

Anticipation of such a new awareness may have been in the minds of those who originally drafted paragraph 111, because it puts certain basic things quite straight. Women should be an integral part of:

— defining the objectives and modes of development,

— developing strategies and measures for their implementation,

— political processes, with an equal share of power in guiding development efforts.

This paragraph also speaks about "alternative development objectives and strategies" which women could and should identify and which others (males!) should support. And, of special importance, it stresses the importance of "special measures ... to enhance women's autonomy" so that they can come into the mainstream of the development process on an equal footing with men.

There are almost 140 paragraphs in this chapter on Development, the most extensive chapter in the whole FLS document. In these paragraphs are incorporated everything possible concerning women and development, all possible needs, plans, aspirations and wishes. Worries about the detrimental consequences of macro-level development on the everyday life of women, and about the risks of increasing women's workload even further, are less clearly expressed. The need to share family responsibilities more evenly between men and women, and between the family and society, is repeated in many connections throughout this chapter.

A universal problem for women is the recognition of unpaid labour in agriculture, trade, households and neighbourhoods, its value and the limitations it imposes on the opportunities for women to participate in education, paid labour, political activities etc. It was problematic also for the drafters of the FLS, where it is now discussed in many paragraphs of various chapters.

Women's informal and invisible economic contributions are discussed first as part of the equality strategies, where it is stipulated that:

— the sharing of domestic responsibilities by all members of the family, and equal recognition of women's informal and invisible economic contributions, should be developed as complementary strategies for the elimination of women's secondary status (paragraph 59).

— careful attention should be paid (in marriage agreements) to the equal participation and valuation of both partners so that the value of housework is considered the equivalent of financial contributions (paragraph 73).

In Chapter II (Development) this problematique is also discussed in several paragraphs:

— the unremunerated contributions of women to all aspects and sectors of development should be recognized, and efforts made to measure and reflect those contributions in national accounts and economic statistics and in the gross national product. Concrete steps should be taken to quantify the unremunerated contributions of women in agriculture, food pro-

duction, reproduction and household activities (paragraph 120).

The measuring of unpaid labour, and its inclusion in national statistics, was very well-defined already in the Mexico
Plan of Action — it was set then as a target to be achieved by
1980:

— Recognition of the economic value of women's work in
the home, in domestic food production and marketing, and
voluntary activities not traditionally remunerated.

The issue was actually discussed more comprehensively in
the Mexico Plan of Action than in the Nairobi FLS 10 years
later. There were fairly specific recommendations
(paragraph 168) as to how, in research and data collection,
special efforts should be made to measure:

(a) the participation of women in local and national planning and policy-making in all sectors of national life;

(b) the extent of women's activities in food production (cash
crop and subsistence agriculture), in water and fuel supply, in
marketing and in transportation;

(c) the economic and social contribution of housework and
other domestic chores, handicrafts and other home-based
economic activities;

(d) the effect on the national economy of women's activities
as consumers of goods and services;

(e) the relative time spent on economic and household activities and on leisure by girls and women compared with
boys and men;

(f) the quality of life (e.g. job satisfaction, income situation,
family characteristics and use of leisure time).

It is indeed a pity that recommendations concerning this
kind of concrete, and immensely important, issue are not
more precise and demanding in the FLS. However, quite a
lot of work has been done on the lines of the Mexico recommendations, especially by the International Research and
Training Institute for the Advancement of Women
(INSTRAW) and by some governments (e.g. Housework Survey in Finland, 1980).

Full recognition of the so-called non-monetarized sections
of national economies, including particularly the unpaid
work of women for their families, would mean a profound
reconstruction of national accounts and statistics. Only then,

however, would become visible the factual components of the quality of life and well-being of families and nations, and the proportional contributions of which all this is composed.

Changing the distribution of labour within families was probably emphasized primarily by Northern women in Nairobi, and it has therefore a somewhat unfortunate formulation in the several places where it is mentioned. "Sharing the parental responsibilities" limits the issue to concern only with child care duties, contrary to the more general formula of family responsibilities. The latter formula could be understood also to mean changing the distribution of labour in such family responsibilities which are performed outside the home, like the collection of wood and water. Changing the distribution of labour in these kinds of duties is not even hinted at in the FLS.

What do the Strategies say about development co-operation between the countries of North and South, and about foreign aid? At the beginning of the chapter the blame for worsening problems in developing countries is put on "the reduction in international co-operation, particularly the inadequate flow of official development assistance and the growing trade protectionism in the developed countries". But otherwise there are rather few recommendations directly concerning development co-operation. Concrete demands are made to increase support to the United Nations Development Fund for Women (UNIFEM) and to the International Research and Training Institute for the Advancement of Women (INSTRAW).

Quantitative increases in development assistance are not much in focus in the FLS. The whole chapter on Development strongly emphasizes the need to improve its quality, and that of development co-operation as well. The emphasis has clearly shifted from quantity to quality, and that is certainly in the interests of women. Perhaps this also reflects the disillusionment of developing countries with regard to the altruism of development assistance by the rich. It has become too obvious, revealed too many times, that development co-operation on the part of rich countries is often only a camouflage for their own political and economic interests.

The Strategies strongly emphasize self-reliance — that of women as well as that of their countries. Self-reliance of women and of the country are seen as mutually enhancing; economic independence for a country is as important as personal income for a woman. Governments, international organizations and voluntary agencies are urged to intensify their efforts to enhance the self-reliance of women in a viable and sustained fashion:

> "Because economic independence is a necessary pre-condition for self-reliance, such efforts should above all be focused on increasing women's access to gainful activities" (paragraph 113). Governments "should also support local research activities and local experts to identify mechanisms for the advancement of women, focusing on the self-reliant, self-sustaining and self-generating social, economic and political development of women" (paragraph 130).

Important policy guidance is given, especially in paragraph 114. First, particular institutions at local, national, regional and international levels should be established to incorporate women's issues in development. "Effective participation of women in development should be integrated in the formulation and implementation of mainstream programmes and projects, and should not be confined solely to statements of intent within plans or to small-scale, transitory projects relating to women."

Measures for implementation of the basic strategies at national level are divided in this chapter into areas for specific action:
— Employment
— Health
— Education
— Food, water and agriculture
— Industry
— Trade and commercial services
— Housing, settlement, community development and transport
— Energy
— Environment
— Social services.

So we see that the Forward-looking Strategies cover most of the areas of international development strategies in general. This should, of course, go without saying, since women make up half of humanity — a half which should be represented and heard on each and every issue.

The huge number of recommendations, instructions and guidelines included in the FLS chapter on Development and its sub-chapters constitute another development strategy, in addition to the International Development Strategy for the Third Development Decade of the United Nations. The IDS for the 1980s, itself, does not incorporate the Mexico Plan of Action of the IWY, or the Copenhagen Programme of Action for the Second Half of the UNDW, as it does the main substance of most of the other Plans of Actions and Programmes adopted in the major World Conferences of the 1970s. This is, once again, an indication of the lack of attention to women's half of humanity in the defining and planning of development for humanity as such.

There is thus all the more reason to consider the Nairobi Forward-looking Strategies, and especially its second chapter on Development, as another international development strategy or at least as a complement to the IDS. Since the FLS looks as far as the year 2000 it should have a decisive impact also on forthcoming international development strategies and the work of international as well as national development agencies.

Peace

FLS Chapter III on Peace is somewhat confusing because it is a mixture of the different elements — the usual UN political terminology together with more feminine language. It has been said that, during the Nairobi Conference, so-called security policy experts — mostly men — in various delegations were careful to ensure that the fixed formulations of their governments' security policy positions were correctly incorporated into the text. These same experts were not interested at all in the very important new ideas which women delegates included in the text and which really give a new impetus to the approach of the FLS.

An important connotation in this chapter is the specific focus on the UN Charter and its principle that governments should refrain from the threat or use of force in international relations. This is commensurate with the thinking of women, since it implies outlawing war once and for all. The Final Document of the Tenth Special Session of the UN General Assembly on Disarmament, 1978, is also explicit in its language.[4]

The important point of departure is defined already in the Introduction, paragraph 13, where the concept of Peace is defined both as absence of war and direct violence and as absence of structural violence, as peace researchers have formulated it. The FLS thus adopts the concept of positive peace instead of negative peace. But this concept is also expanded in an extremely important way for women; it makes it clear that violence at all levels, personal, social and international, stems from the same roots and should be seen as indications of the same phenomenon. Sustainable peace cannot be achieved without eliminating violence at all levels, including violence against women. This approach is well clarified in paragraphs 257 and 258:

"The questions of women and peace, and the meaning of peace for women, cannot be separated from the broader question of relationships between women and men in all spheres of life and in the family". And:

"Violence against women exists in various forms in everyday life in all societies. Women are beaten, mutilated, burned, sexually abused and raped. Such violence is a major obstacle to the achievement of peace and the other objectives of the Decade and should be given special attention. Women victims of violence should be given particular attention and comprehensive assistance. To this end, legal measures should be formulated to prevent violence and to assist women victims. National machinery should be established in order to deal with the question of violence against women within the family and society. Preventive policies should be elaborated, and institutionalized forms of assistance to women victims provided."

This approach expands the perspective of peace to cover the whole of society and culture, not only relationships between states or opponent parties within societies. Violence against women at the personal level and within families is a universal phenomenon, and as such is of global concern to all women. Military values and militarized masculinity perpetuate this kind of violence, which is directly linked to the persistence of military institutions and the use of violence and force in international relations.

The Nairobi Forward-looking Strategies paper is the first unanimously adopted intergovernmental document in which the concept of violence is defined in a comprehensive way, and where the links between use of violence at personal and international levels are recognized.

It is interesting to note some 'feminist' interpretations of the prevailing formulations in the FLS, for example the concept of confidence-building, which is used in the sense of confidence between nations and people, and not between the militaries as usually in official negotiations. Paragraph 241 emphasizes the importance of women joining hands and supporting each other across national borders:

"It is essential that women support and encourage each other in their initiatives and action relating either to universal issues, such as disarmament and the development of confidence-building measures between nations and people, or to specific conflict situations between or within States."

The third feminist emphasis in this chapter can be seen in the fairly extensive discussion about education for peace. It is dealt with both in basic strategies and measures at the national level, and also in Chapter V concerning international and regional co-operation (paragraphs 344, 354, 355). In paragraph 256 it is stipulated:

"Women of the world, together with men, should, as informal educators and socialization agents, play a special role in the process of bringing up younger generations in an atmosphere of compassion, tolerance, mutual concern and trust, with an awareness that all people belong to the same world community. Such education should be part of all formal and informal educational processes, as well as of communications, information and mass-media systems."

The substance and means of peace education are elaborated in
a special subsection (paragraphs 272-276):

> "Governments, non-governmental organizations,
> women's groups and the mass media should encourage
> women to engage in efforts to promote education for peace
> in the family, neighbourhood and community. The skills
> and talents of women artists, journalists, writers, educa-
> tors and civic leaders can contribute to promoting ideas of
> peace if encouraged, facilitated and supported.
>
> "... suitable concrete action should be taken to discourage
> the provision of children with games and publications and
> other media promoting the notion of favouring war, ag-
> gression, cruelty, excessive desire for power and other
> forms of violence, within the broad processes of the prepa-
> ration of society for life in Peace." Materials for peace edu-
> cation "should include case studies of peaceful settlements
> of disputes, nonviolent movements and passive resistance
> and the recognition of peace-seeking individuals".

(Interestingly enough, the additional words at this point in
the draft, "rather than the glorification of war heroes", were
deleted in the last stage!)

Much attention is given to women's access to information
and knowledge of the main problems in contemporary international relations as a means of contributing to their ability to influence these issues:

> "All existing obstacles and discriminatory practices re-
> garding women's civil and political education should be
> removed."

An interesting new point is made in this connection:

> "Opportunities should be provided for women to organize
> and choose studies, training programmes and seminars
> related to peace, disarmament, education for peace and the
> peaceful settlement of disputes."

This could be taken to mean that women should have the
right and the opportunity to organize their studies by themselves and according to their own views and perceptions of
reality, possibly differently from the way in which these
issues are taught in established schools and universities.

Another important recommendation concerns women in peace research (paragraph 276):

"The participation of women in peace research, including research on women and peace, should be encouraged. Existing barriers to women researchers should be removed and appropriate resources provided for peace researchers. Co-operation amongst peace researchers, government officials, non-governmental organizations and activists should be encouraged and fostered."

The frequently patronizing attitude towards women, prominent in this chapter, is contradictory to the whole meaning of the FLS. Formulations such as "the mass media should encourage women" or "governments should mobilize women to overcome social apathy and helplessness", and even "non-governmental organizations should provide opportunities for women" all give the impression that women have been passive and reluctant to work and educate for peace.

This is, indeed, a totally false picture of reality, since in many countries women are the most active proponents of peace and peace education. During the UN Decade for Women, a specific women's peace movement has developed which has had a new, creative impact on peace activities throughout the world. And everywhere it is women who have been the proponents and developers of peace education at all levels. So in this respect, even more than in others, the FLS should demand that governments listen to women and take their views into consideration, instead of patronizing them as if they were really subordinate objects.

International and regional co-operation

The last two chapters of the FLS deal with areas of special concern, and international and regional co-operation. The areas of special concern include women in areas affected by drought, urban poor women, elderly women, young women, abused and destitute women, victims of trafficking and involuntary prostitution, women deprived of their traditional means of livelihood (meaning in fact environmental haz-

ards particularly affecting women), women as sole supporters
of families, physically and mentally disabled women,
women in detention, refugee and displaced women and
children, migrant women and minority and "indigenous"
women.

Chapter V on International and Regional Co-operation
records existing possibilities and alternative ways of international co-operation rather than definite, concrete proposals. It does not propose any new organs or institutions to be
established for the advancement of women, or make any
definite proposals about when, and in what ways, the monitoring and follow-up of the Nairobi decisions are supposed to
take place.

Concrete recommendations are made for governments to
support and strengthen existing organs and institutions of
the UN System, such as the Branch for the Advancement of
Women in the Centre for Social Development and Humanitarian Affairs (CSDHA) of the Department of International
Economic and Social Affairs (DIESA). Specific institutions
such as the International Research and Training Institute
for the Advancement of Women (INSTRAW) and the
United Nations Development Fund for Women (UNIFEM)
should be supported, and resources allocated for them
increased.

No decision was taken to hold another United Nations
world conference on women; it was recommended only that
"at least one world conference be held during the period between 1985 and the year 2000". There are, however, a few
very important and concrete proposals about the coordination
and follow-up of the implementation of the Forward-looking
Strategies within the UN System itself. It was decided that:

— the preparations of new instruments and strategies such
as the overall strategies for international development (i.e.
the new international development strategy for the fourth
UN Development Decade) should pay specific, appropriate attention to the advancement of women;

— future medium-term plans of the United Nations and the
Specialized Agencies should contain intersectoral presenta-
tions of the various programmes dealing with issues of concern to women;

— the Secretary-General should take the initiative in formulating a System-wide medium-term plan for women and development.

These recommendations may, again, seem to be very bureaucratic and alienating procedures but, as we shall see later in this book, they commit the entire intergovernmental system to the implementation of the Nairobi Forward-looking Strategies for the Advancement of Women.

The Forward-looking Strategies: advantages and constraints

We have seen earlier that there are a lot of new, progressive ideas in the FLS; many of these were adopted for the first time ever as part of an intergovernmental programme.

In fact, the FLS redefine the goals of both development and peace policies internationally. Equality and well-being of people are set as primary goals of development instead of economic growth, industrialization and expansion of trade and business. In the field of peace the FLS see security in a comprehensive way; they define peace as progress towards elimination of all kinds of violence, physical as well as structural, including violence against women. It is here that development and peace are interlinked. Development towards better justice and equality is a way of eliminating the causes of conflict and thus building better foundations for lasting peace.

If one tries to abstract any paramount general strategies from the FLS, they are the same as those which were highlighted also in the World Survey on the Role of Women in Development. The most important strategy to advance the situation for women is:
— to see to it that the access of women to education at all levels and all fields of education and training really becomes equal with that of men in all schools and institutions, and that the obstacles faced by women be removed.

In order to redirect development in general to correspond with women's views and aspirations in all countries it is necessary:
— that women have access to power and to participation in designing, planning and decision-making on development in all walks of life and at all levels of society, on an equal

footing with men. Achieving a balance between male and female participation in decision-making is the most important way in which to develop a better balance in life and the more humane progress of societies in general.

As a whole the FLS constitute a broadly-based document with many political mandates, confusing perhaps to a reader unfamiliar with United Nations language but containing many advances adopted by consensus. Some feminist activists have expressed concern that more accent was not put on suggestions that women "should organize themselves", "take the opportunities to do ..." or declare that women "have the right to oppose their governments", instead of using language such as women "should be encouraged and mobilized, "being provided for" or "given the right to disagree."

Since delegates are representatives of their governments, they obviously have to follow instructions. However, it is important to work towards ensuring a thorough training for delegates, so that they become familiar with the many points arising out of the analysis of the real situation which is being carried out by women's research. Such training could assist women delegates to resist being so easily co-opted by a system dominated by men.

Increased participation of women in decision-making at all levels is the prime aim of the FLS. But the experience of the Nairobi Conference, and the quality of the FLS document, are obvious examples of the importance of the level of awareness of women in decision-making. It is not enough simply to have more women in the decision-making bodies; it is decisively important that they develop their awareness and knowledge as women, in order to acquire growing competence in representing, authentically, the female half of humanity.

This need to arouse women's awareness throughout the world is vaguely implicit in the FLS; it is not explicitly expressed anywhere. The need for empowerment of women is hidden between the lines here and there. The more equal participation of women is seen primarily within the framework of ordinary "equality thinking", i.e. as participation of women within the established system as such, without introducing any profound changes.

In fact the FLS document, by its very nature, is another intergovernmental document reflecting governmental approaches towards women in the middle of the 1980s. As it is now it could, and should, be used effectively to push governments to implement at least what they have unanimously agreed to do in the document, to require them to keep their promises. Governments everywhere need to be pushed, and even pressurized, to implement their international decisions, because otherwise they are likely to forget what they have agreed. The implementation of UN decisions thus rely heavily on active citizens in each country.

There are many aids produced for us as citizens to fulfil our task in controlling our governments' performance in implementing the FLS. The document has been translated into national languages in many countries where none of the official UN languages is spoken. Indeed, translation is the very first step for governments, in order to make it accessible to women in their countries. Where it is not done, this should be the first demand upon the government. If that does not work, women should find ways and means to do it themselves.

The International Women's Tribune Center in New York has produced an excellent community action guide entitled *It's Our Move Now* to help women in all countries to study the FLS and to use the document for pressurizing their governments, legislative bodies, administrations, employers, etc. to implement its provisions.[5]

The FLS give appropriate substance also to universities, colleges and other institutions of learning and research, to work on, study, analyze and learn how to use it. Learning to use this UN document will at the same time teach women to use other UN documents as well, and to understand the whole idea of international governmental co-operation and what sense it makes from the citizen's point of view. Special programmes and study guides for this purpose have been prepared in many countries.

And last but perhaps most important is the role of the women's movement and women's organizations in all countries: to work with women, promote awareness-raising processes, and encourage and strengthen women in assuming their legitimate position as sovereign citizens of their countries.

Women's organizations and movements should not, however, stop at the Nairobi Forward-looking Strategies and their provisions — the aims which governments were able to adopt together. They must set their goals independently, and go beyond the FLS in practice. The visions and aims of DAWN and other non-governmental groups and researchers give impetus to the women's movement to set its own goals and aspirations.

> "A time has come when, instead of waiting for benefits from society or government or development itself to reach them or to be given to them, women themselves will have to take power and make the opportunities happen."

These are the bold words from the Report of the International Workshop on Feminist Ideology and Structures in the First Half of the Decade for Women, organized in Bangkok, Thailand, in 1979 by the Asian and Pacific Centre for Women and Development.[6]

Even if the FLS as a document does not satisfy our most progressive perspectives and aspirations, it is a document which we must use effectively. It can be used as leverage to turn the UN System in the direction in which we would like it to go. In later chapters we shall study what is going on in the UN System to implement the FLS, and what is being planned for forthcoming years in order to make the Strategies work. This is the process which we should all try to follow as closely as possible in order to monitor also the participation and positions taken by our own governments in various bodies of the United Nations System.

Notes

1 The Nairobi Forward-looking Strategies for the Advancement of Women. Published by UN Department of Public Information, New York.

2 Review and Appraisal of progress achieved and obstacles encountered at the national level in the realization of the goals and objectives of the United Nations Decade for Women: Equality, Development and Peace. Report of the Secretary-General, A/CONF.116.5 and Addenda 1-14. Also A/CONF.116/28, Rev.1, Sales No.E.85.IV.10.

3 Declaration of Mexico: Plans of Action, United Nations New York, December 1975. And Report of the World Conference of the United Nations Decade for Women: Equality-Development-Peace, Copenhagen. United Nations, New York, 1980.

4 Final Document, Special Session of the General Assembly on Disarmament, 1978, DPI/679 — 40708, February 1981, United Nations, New York.

5 *It's Our Move Now.* A Community Action Guide to the UN Nairobi Forward-looking Strategies for the Advancement of Women. International Women's Tribune Center, 777 United Nations Plaza, New York, NY 10017.

6 *Developing Strategies for the Future Feminist Perspectives.* (Contains the reports of the workshops in Bangkok in 1979 and at Stony Point, New York, 1980.) Distributed by the International Women's Center, New York.

4.

The United Nations Decade for Women, 1976-1985

The Declaration and Adoption of IWY:
The three formative years, 1972 -1974

We should perhaps look also at the process which led to the decision on the UN Decade for Women, with all its ramifications. The process started to mature at the beginning of the 1970's. Two primary factors behind this development were, without doubt, the emergence of a new — both in time and substance — phase of the international women's movement, and the aggravation of two major international problems, population and food, at that time. These huge problems finally forced the UN System to realize that women in developing countries were the key factor in the solution to them.

It is woman who gives birth; her motivation and the possibilities she has to limit the number of her children are therefore crucial elements in the solution of population problems. In Africa it is the woman who, by her personal contribution in the form of labour, provides the staple food for her family. Thus, these two major basic problems — food and population — have their roots in the way she lives. Women have to reconcile their work (subsistence farming, collecting wood and carrying water for the essential needs of daily life) with the time spent delivering and nurturing children. Development aimed at satisfaction of basic needs depends upon the limited resources and unrealized potential of women. But before this aspect of the situation was clearly perceived, the Second Development Decade of the 1970's was far advanced.

International Women's Year, 1975

An oral tradition in the UN family says that the seeds of IWY came from Finland. A non-governmental organization, the Women's International Democractic Federation, first proposed the declaration of a women's year, and WIDF's president then was a prominent Finnish parliamentarian, Hertta Kuusinen. Representing her organization as an observer at the 1972 session of the UN Commission on the Status of Women, Ms. Kuusinen, together with a number of other NGO observers, drafted a proposal which she convinced the Romanian representative on the Commission to present. The Finnish government representative at that time, Helvi Sipilä, seconded the proposal and, on Leap Year Day in 1972, the Commission decided to recommend to the General Assembly the declaration of 1975 as International Women's Year.

Thus, IWY is one example of an NGO initiative taken up by the UN System — one which on this occasion exceeded all expectations, developing into a process with dimensions and repercussions such as the initiators had hardly dared to dream of.

The UN General Assembly was less enthusiastic about the idea of IWY when the recommendation came up in the Third Committee in November 1972. This scepticism was partly due to the proliferation of so-called "theme" years (which had already been somewhat numerous) and partly to doubts as to the wisdom of singling women's issues out for special attention. The recommendation was nevertheless unanimously adopted in December 1972.

By then, the position of women in the UN Secretariat had also become an issue. The proportion of women occupying senior posts was very low, and no woman so far had been appointed to any top job. Calls to rectify this situation were considered by the then new Secretary-General, Kurt Waldheim, sufficiently disturbing to warrant a search for competent women candidates to fill several key vacancies. Helvi Sipilä, appointed in the autumn of 1972, was the UN's first female Assistant Secretary-General.

The decision to celebrate 1975 as International Women's Year, and the appointment of the first female Assistant Secretary-General in the same year, were a mere coincidence. However, both events flagged the beginning of a new "women's era" in the UN, and the emergence of the new women's movement in Western countries.

The advance influence of the IWY

Few doubt that IWY was the most successful of the many theme years the UN had held thus far. It came at a time when many other factors were converging in the same direction; the problems of women had finally to be taken seriously, and their role in the development of each and every country recognized. IWY thus became a framework within which these issues could be the subject of global attention and, at the same time, it highlighted the forgotten dimensions of many issues in a way which would not otherwise have been possible.

IWY, in fact, had significant influence before it even began. Preparations for the World Population Conference (1974) were already well under way when the decision on IWY was taken, and — hard though it is to believe — gave no recognition to women's role in population questions. This alarmed a number of NGOs and caught the attention of the new Assistant Secretary-General. Early in 1974 these NGOs, together with Ms. Sipilä's Division for Social Development and Humanitarian Affairs, organized an unofficial preparatory meeting, the *International Forum on the Role of Women in Population and Development*, attended by a prominent female personality from each of 116 countries.

This meeting proved to be an eye-opening event, after which it was no longer possible to ignore the link between women and population. Many of the women who participated in that 'lobbying' meeting were later on the delegations of their respective countries to the *World Population Conference* in Bucharest in August 1974. Thanks in no small measure to their efforts, the World Population Plan of Action gave appropriate recognition to the importance of population policies to women and to the role women had to play in these issues. It was realized that no population policy could be effective without the involvement of women, and unless due consideration be given to their interests.

Another important conference was held in 1974 — the *World Food Conference,* which took place in Rome. Partly due to interest generated by the upcoming IWY, and partly to a slowly-emerging general awareness of the vital contribution made by women to world food supplies, it was recognized that the world food situation could not be improved without full integration of women into the policies decided upon. Again, NGOs played a prominent role in addressing this issue at the Rome Conference.

Extensive preparations for IWY were launched in most UN Member states and in the Specialized Agencies of the UN System. Regional preparatory conferences were organized by all UN Economic Commissions, and the process culminated in the World Conference of the IWY in mid-1975, in Mexico. The decision-making bodies of most of the UN agencies and organs approved specific resolutions in those of their fields of competence in which women's aspects had obvious relevance. IWY was the first of the UN theme years for which extensive preparations were undertaken at all levels: national, regional and international.

The World Plan of Action of the IWY[1]

The decision to organize a world IWY conference was taken somewhat tardily. It was only a year before, in the spring of 1974, that ECOSOC had passed a resolution to that effect. The time available for preparatory work was, therefore, extremely short compared with that available for many other such conferences. (The World Population Conference, for example, was prepared over a period of almost three years.)

It was customary for a comprehensive plan of action to be prepared for the world conferences of the 1970's. This would take place in several stages so that drafts could be sent to Member States for comments, following receipt of which revised drafts were prepared. In this way the views of governments were rather fully incorporated in the conference documents. There was no time for the draft plan of action for the women's conference to be drawn up in this way. It was the first such document the world had seen to concentrate specifically on problems and concerns of women, covering all possible aspects of their lives from food, health and education to family planning and political participation. Work on it had to be limited to the Secretariat and a small preparatory committee of 23 Member States, but the substance for the World Plan of Action could be drawn from recommendations and resolutions adopted on women's issues in the various UN bodies over the preceding thirty years.

Delegations of 133 governments took part in the Mexico City Conference. They represented countries with very different levels of development and a wide variety of cultures, traditions and customs. Since Member States had had no opportunity to express their views and aspirations with regard to the World Plan of Action in advance, all these were poured out at the Conference itself. The original draft contained 205 paragraphs; participants proposed almost 900 amendments and additions. In a two-week conference it was impossible to handle so many proposals, and the major part of the Plan of Action was thus adopted as it had been drafted.

Irrespective of these problems, the WPA became a document of the utmost importance. The impact of its aims and obligations concerning development was already felt in the latter part of the 1970's in member countries and the UN System. Annexed to the WPA were separate Regional Plans of Action for Asia and Africa (prepared and adopted beforehand by the regional preparatory conferences). Covering more geographically-limited (and thus more unified) areas, they are, by nature, more specific and concrete than is the WPA.

As adopted, the World Plan of Action for the Implementation of the Objectives of IWY sets targets and proposes actions at both national and international levels for the decade 1976-1985. For the first half of the Decade, until 1980, these were specific and concrete. It was proposed that a second world conference be organized in 1980 to review and appraise implementation.

In December of the same year the recommendations of the World Conference were approved by the UN General Assembly, which also declared 1976-1985 as the *UN Decade for Women*, with the same themes selected for IWY: Equality, Development, Peace. Throughout the Decade, governments, intergovernmental organizations (in particular the UN agencies), non-governmental organizations and other institutions and communities around the world would strive to implement the WPA.

The Mid-Decade Conference in Copenhagen, 1980

In accordance with the decision in Mexico, a second world conference was organised in Copenhagen in 1980, to review and appraise to what extent the targets set in the WPA had been attained during the first half of the UN Decade for Women and to prepare a more precise Plan of Action for the remainder of the Decade.[2]

One effect of the WPA was that the female perspective was recognized in some of the other world conferences of the 1970's and in resolutions adopted by the Specialized Agencies. In the UN General Assembly women's issues were no longer discussed only in the Third Comittee (Social and Humanitarian) but also in others, notably the Second Committee (Economic Co-operation and Development). This was positive indication of unfolding awareness that attempts to promote the status of women are little more than mere window-dressing unless the appropriate material basis is created.

The UN Decade for Women also speeded up work on the *Convention on the Elimination of All Forms of Discrimination against Women,* the final text of which was adopted by the General Assembly in 1979.[3] Member States were then invited to sign and ratify it in due course, and 60 of them signed it during the Copenhagen Conference.

During the first five years of the Decade the UN System undertook systematic collection of data on the situation and circumstances of women all over the world, thereby making available a mass of new, up-to-date background material. The approaching conference also accelerated preparation and implementation of national programmes to ensure equality between men and women.

The redefined Plan of Action for the second part of the Decade (1980-1985) was adopted in Copenhagen. In addition to the overall themes of the Decade, the document focuses especially on problems of employment, health and education from the women's viewpoint. A decision was taken to convene a third world conference, in 1985, to review and appraise achievements over the Decade as a whole, and to draw up guidelines for the future.

Hopes and disappointments

The atmosphere at, and passions aroused by, the World Conference in Mexico City reflected not only the issues on the agenda but also the historical background against which the conference took place, and the prevailing world situation. It was the first UN conference in which a majority (73%) of delegates were women, and where as many as 113 delegations were headed by a woman. (Although it should be noted that the proportion of men among delegates was higher (27%) than is the usual proportion of women at other UN conferences!)

Thus, hopes and expectations were high — one might even say exaggerated or over-enthusiastic — and this was one reason for the flood of amendments and resolutions. To participate as a delegate in the Conference was, in itself, a great experience for many women, most of whom had no previous experience and knowledge of the proceedings of such intergovernmental gatherings. In such circumstances, the outcome of the Conference was a good one and, indeed, constituted a landmark.

Many participants' hopes and expectations were dashed in Copenhagen too, due in no small measure to the approaches adopted by the traditional political blocs. Market economy countries stressed equality between men and women as the key factor in the struggle to improve the latter's status, while developing countries considered overall acceleration of economic and social development the most important thing from the point of view of both women and men; they took the view that Western-type equality could only become a reality when the basic material needs of all people had been satisfied. Socialist states held that equality between men and women was already a fact of life in those countries, and therefore emphasized the same political issues they stressed in other UN fora.

As has been pointed out elsewhere, these characteristic differences of opinion lead one to ask whether the real concerns of women are heard in such intergovernmental conferences. Even when the majority of delegates are women, delegations will express their official government line — and in how many countries does official policy really take account of women's views and rights?

General political issues came to the forefront in Copenhagen, those same issues (Palestine, Zionism, racial discrimination, etc.) which governments were disputing *ad infinitum* elsewhere. Big powers were playing their power game, developing countries fought for more equitable international trade and a new international economic order. Even when greater emphasis was placed by some Western governments on questions of sexual equality, this was construed as a useful ploy to avoid discussion of politically-difficult issues! The fact that a delegation had a female majority did not, therefore, necessarily ensure that it would give priority to other concerns of women.

Parallel conferences as free fora

As a result, the true voice of women was all the more clearly audible at the parallel NGO conferences: the *IWY Tribune* in Mexico City and the *NGO Forum* in Copenhagen. While the number of official delegates to both governmental conferences was around 1,200, there were some 4,000 participants at the NGO meeting in Mexico City and some 7,000 at that in Copenhagen — almost all of them women.

The fact that the two parallel conferences gathered such unforeseen numbers (more than at any previous UN world conference) proved more than anything else that women all over the world are active and interested in their own issues. In the literally hundreds of meetings, panels, symposia, free gatherings, etc. which took place under the auspices of these parallel conferences, women really spoke out about their problems, fears and worries. Of course, there were disputes and disagreements, but the ability of women to communicate and to meet as sisters, irrespective of differences of political and cultural backgrounds, was amply demonstrated.

Many groups and individuals went to parallel conferences with the hope of being able to influence the resolutions of the official, intergovernmental conference. On the spot, however, this is very difficult and chances are rare. Non-governmental organizations or independent groups have to master lobbying techniques, and understand UN conference procedures clearly, in order to make an impact on the official debates. This was a bitter lesson for many parallel conference participants.

It is worth repeating that the best way to influence a government's policy is beforehand, back home in each country, through measures such as lobbying, political pressure, contacts with influential persons, etc. International co-operation and coordination between national groups in different countries is needed in order to bring simultaneous pressure on governments in a number of countries, thereby enhancing chances of success at the intergovernmental level.

However, the lessons were learned, and had been useful, as we realized in Nairobi in 1985. The experiences of the Nairobi Conference proved how extensive and thoroughgoing had been this process, which actually started in Mexico City and has continued ever since in various forms (see Chapter 1).

Notes

[1]   Declaration of Mexico — Plan of Action. United Nations, New York, December 1975.

[2]   Report of the World Conference of the United Nations Decade for Women : Equality-Development-Peace (Copenhagen). United Nations, New York, 1980.

[3]   Convention on the Elimination of All Forms of Discrimination Against Women. United Nations, New York, 1979 (see Annex 1).

5.
The Importance of
Other World Conferences

The conferences on women in Mexico City and Copenhagen were part of the series of world conferences convened by the UN System during the Second Development Decade (the 1970's) and continuing in the 1980's. Thus, they were not unique in themselves.

The purpose of the series was to map out the global situation in various specific problem areas, and to draw up long-term plans of action in the respective fields. The integration of women, their contributions and problems, came to the fore in several conferences other than those in Mexico and Denmark. This can be explained by the obligations of International Women's Year and the UN Decade for Women; it was, quite simply, no longer possible to ignore women's links to the substantive areas under consideration. It is also the reason why the impact of IWY and the Decade was greater than that of any other UN theme year or decade.

The logic of world conferences

At the request of the UN Department of International Economic and Social Affairs, researcher Ingrid Palmer undertook an assessment of the ways in which women's role in the development process was approached and analysed in 12 world conferences held during the 1970's.[1] Her report was published as a background document for the World Conference of the UN Decade for Women held in Copenhagen in 1980. It begins with a general observation: women's issues in fact received more attention at the *World Population Conference*

and the *World Food Conference*, held immediately before the
1975 IWY, than in those held immediately after IWY and
the adoption of the World Plan of Action to implement its
objectives. However, by the end of the 1970's, women's issues
were again attracting increased attention.

The emphasis at the beginning of the decade on the role
of women in connection with population and food problems
(without which it would have been impossible to get a true
picture of either, let alone come up with ideas to solve them)
no doubt paved the way to recognition of women's role in development as a whole. However, in other conferences, where
women's links were less obvious (or not acknowledged),
recognition of women remained accidental and it was only
towards the end of the 1970's — when the impact of the
WPA and the obligations of the Decade began to be felt —
that greater attention was again focused on the feminine aspects of the matters under discussion.

Ingrid Palmer's report sheds interesting light on some of
the factors which proved decisive in determining whether
or not women's aspects came out at various conferences (see
list of World Conferences, Annex 4).

The Population and Food Conferences

As already noted, it was these two conferences which first directed the spotlight onto women's issues, and not only because of the very close links of women to the subjects under
study. The fact that the newly-appointed Assistant Secretary-
General, Helvi Sipilä, had thoroughly studied the relationship between the status of women and family planning and,
as one of her first tasks, drew the attention of those concerned with the preparatory process for the Population Conference to the role of women in this connection, was as crucial a factor as the lobbying conference she helped to organize, together with a number of US NGOs, at the beginning of 1974.

Practical preparations and administration of the World
Food Conference were in the hands of the UN Food and
Agriculture Organization. For many years FAO had had an
extremely efficient nutrition section, staffed mainly by

women. They were well aware of the vital role of women in food production, especially in Africa, and ensured that this was adequately covered in the conference documents. At the time of the WFC itself an NGO group organized a parallel meeting, also in Rome, which succeeded in influencing the official Conference. It is important to note that the members of this group had already been active beforehand, in their home countries, endeavouring to influence preparations at the national level.

As a consequence the Conference recognized the part played by women in food production, processing and marketing, in family nutrition, in decisions on family size, etc. and the need to involve them fully in the process of rural development and extension services. Governments were urged to involve women fully in the decision-making machinery for food production and nutrition, and to give women equal access with men to education and training in agricultural technology, marketing and distribution techniques. Ingrid Palmer states that "taken together, this set of resolutions is remarkable for its sensitivity to women's issues".

Other world conferences

The situation was completely different with HABITAT, the *United Nations Conference on Human Settlements*, held in Vancouver in 1976. Ingrid Palmer summarised her conclusions on this Conference by saying it "failed to state clearly how the environment had a special impact on women's domestic work, and that improvements therein were a precondition for women's effective use of access to other economic and social opportunities. Its reference to the special problems of the young, the aged and the handicapped highlighted this omission, since women currently serve as the last refuge for these vulnerable groups."

The *World Conference on Employment, Income Distribution, Social Progress and the International Division of Labour,* in 1976, launched the concept of 'basic needs' into international development discussions. It acknowledged that rural women, especially, were "rather overworked than underemployed", and that it was hypocritical to stress the importance of full participation of women in public affairs when they "have little or no free time and have a poor resource base from which to represent their claims on communal effort". The great contribution of this Conference was its analysis and appraisal of basic needs delivery systems, which pays appropriate tribute to the role of women. As observed by Ingrid Palmer, the Employment Conference was also the first forum where women's special interests, and the conflict between social and economic investments, were raised by the international community.

The *Conference on Economic Co-operation among Developing Countries* in 1976, the *Water Conference* in 1977, the *Conference on Desertification* the same year, and the *Conference on Technical Cooperation among Developing Countries* in 1978 failed totally to realise that there might be an important women's dimension in these topics, and that its recognition might enhance possibilities of solving some of the problems. It is particularly difficult to understand this omission in respect of the Water Conference, since it is well-known that, over the centuries, women have been and are the basic water supply system in many countries. It is surely obvious, therefore, that the provision of a secure water delivery system will, first and foremost, be of interest to them.

Equally unbelievable is the fact that the *Primary Health Care Conference* held in Alma Ata in 1978 managed to pass resolutions on public participation, food production, proper nutrition, water, sanitation, training and appropriate health technology, without mentioning women. Did not the fact that the universal basic health care system has forever been mothers (whose knowledge and skills have been the basis of family nutrition and hygiene and who have taken care of children and the aged and nurtured the sick when no other services existed) deserve recognition? This Conference "was extraordinary in that it ignored the very substantial sex-differentiated interests in preventive health measures", concludes Ingrid Palmer.

However, the United Nations Steering Committee for the Implementation of the *International Drinking Water Supply and Sanitation Decade* did pay full attention in its work to the problems of women, and incorporated INSTRAW as a full member of the Committee. A task force on women, water supply and sanitation was established, to provide guidelines on future policies in this field with regard to the full participation of women.

Virtually all the conferences lauded the principle of public participation in decision-making, but the *World Conference on Agrarian Reform and Rural Development,* held in Rome in 1979, was the only one to realise that certain pre-conditions had to be met before women could participate effectively, says Dr. Palmer. By calling for women's personal rights in land reform it clearly manifested its understanding of the necessity to examine facts governing exchange and distribution, not only between the various social classes making up a community but also in individual households.

In this Conference the influence of independent NGO groups was visible and far from negligible. The Food Policy Study Group of the International Peace Research Association had been established in connection with the World Food Conference five years earlier, and had continued its work in the intervening period. It was also the initiator of the Rome Declaration Group at the 1979 Conference, distributing alternative information to the delegates and carrying out effective lobbying, in many different areas, before and during the Conference.

The *UN Conference on Science and Technology for Development,* which took place in Vienna in 1979, was somewhat unique in that considerable efforts had already been made during the preparatory process by NGOs and female delegates to the Preparatory Committee to have the women's perspective appropriately incorporated in the texts of the draft document. Almost all this work, however, was in vain, due to active opposition from many delegations, both in the Preparatory Committee and in the Commissions of the Conference itself.

In an ultimate attempt, a couple of Nordic women delegates took the initiative, in mid-Conference, of launching a draft resolution on women, science and technology, drafted so as to oblige all implementing bodies, both national and international, to integrate women into all activities laid out in the Plan of Action of the Conference as adopted. Within a few days the draft attracted quite a number of sponsors among the delegations and, in the concluding plenary, was presented as a joint resolution of the host country, the Nordic countries and a number of developing countries, and unanimously adopted. It calls for the integration and appropriate participation of women in all organs and decision-making bodies which decide on the selection and implementation of science and technology for development, in both Third World and industrialized countries.

Recognition of women — a matter of chance?

Ultimately, then, it seems to have been a matter of mere chance if women's voice was heard in the 'male enclaves' of UN world conferences — even when the women's angle was well-justified and documented. For example, two very substantial background documents on the importance of water issues for women were prepared for the Water Conference by the UN Secretariat and the appropriate unit of FAO, but the Conference ignored these aspects — presumably because there were no active women on the delegations to get them to the discussion table and also, perhaps, because there was little parallel NGO activity on this occasion.

Male-dominated delegations do not seem to take up women's issues in UN conferences, even when they are extensively covered in the conference documentation. Do men fear being branded as eccentric and opportunistic if they support an issue which, traditionally, they have steered clear of?

When at least a few active women have been on the delegations or national preparatory organs for UN conferences, or working for NGOs concerned with the substantive issue, they have generally taken the initiative and — when sufficiently well-versed in UN procedures — have been able to get draft resolutions through all the various stages. A well-argued and well-prepared resolution may well receive support even from male delegates. (See Annex 5: How to prepare a resolution for a UN Conference.)

The case of women and industrialization

One might assume that industrialization is the last field in which anybody would think of taking up the female dimension. However, it is especially important to bring women's aspects and interests into focus at an early stage in the industrialization of developing countries, in order to avoid making the same mistakes already made in industrial societies.

Consideration of the women's angle at UNIDO in the 1970's demonstrates what can happen if there are one or two people to launch an initiative at the right time and in the right place. The Second General Conference of the UN Industrial Development Organization in 1975 adopted the *Lima Declaration and Plan of Action,* designed to apply the principles of the new international economic order in the field of industrialization. In the document, reference was already made to the importance of recognizing the importance of the impact of industrialization on the female section of the population. It also provided that equal access to training for industrial professions be ensured for all, without any discrimination, including on the basis of sex.

The Lima documents were drafted by the Group of 77 (developing countries) in which Ms. Chafika Sellami-Meslem of Algeria saw to it that women's angles were not overlooked. Later a draft resolution was prepared — with inspiration and support from the UN Secretariat — on women and industrialization to further elaborate the relevant provisions of the Lima Plan of Action. It was unanimously adopted at the Ninth Session of the Industrial Development Board a few months after the Lima Conference, in IDB Resolution 44 (IX), 25 April 1975.

This mandated UNIDO to organize, among other things, a workshop in 1978 on the role of women in industrialization in developing countries. The recommendations adopted at the workshop were very much to the point at that stage, and very concrete. They covered discrimination with respect to recruitment, training, wages and promotion; prejudices and attitudinal barriers to women's employment in industry; practices of transnational corporations; contracted-out piecework; basic education; promotion of women's co-operatives in small and medium-sized enterprises; future work by UNIDO in this area; and efforts to unionise women.

This workshop was only the first step in the implementation of the provisions of the IDB resolution, and did not come until three years later. It was therefore necessary to raise the issue again at the Third General Conference of UNIDO which took place in New Delhi in 1980. UNIDO III was to draw up principles and guidelines for industrial development until the year 2000, which made it all the more important to ensure that UNIDO itself and member countries took the interests of womankind into consideration in the process.

A group of women in Helsinki drafted a resolution on women and industrialization and presented it to the Finnish delegation to UNIDO III, which brought it up at the preparatory meeting for the Conference. It gained the support of the other Nordic countries, and at the conference was submitted as a joint initiative by the Nordics and 10 other countries from various regions — the only resolution unanimously adopted at UNIDO III. ID/CONF.4/Res.1 invites UNIDO, *inter alia,* to keep under constant review the impact of the Lima Declaration and Plan of Action on women, and to report regularly on the status of its implementation. It requests that participation of women be promoted on a par with that of men in planning and decision-making.

Time has shown that the resolution did not come a moment too soon, but also that it did not go far enough. The unprecedented expansion of industries, and especially of transnational corporations, in southern Asia, has aggravated many existing problems and created new ones. In 1984 women already outnumbered men in Asia's industrial labour force — although the conditions in which they work are well-nigh appalling.

The report *Women in Development: A Resource Guide for Organization and Action,* published by ISIS (Women's International Information and Communication Service) in 1983,[2] states:

"... women are super-exploited by these enterprises, whose main motivation for hiring women is the higher profits derived from paying women the lower salaries ... The industries well realize the goldmine they have struck with women, who are usually the most willing to work, the easiest to fire and the least likely to unionise. With little or no protection for wages, benefits and work, women are the most abused section of the formal labour force."

In the process of rapid automation the industries in southeast Asia, which for a time brought thousands of women from villages into industrial labour (i.e. into the money economy) are now about to close down and return to their home countries, since cheap labour is not that profitable any more. What then will be the fate of the displaced, out-of-work women? Prostitution? Few among them will return to their native villages.

No resolution adopted in the UN System can take effect unless member governments implement it nationally and monitor implementation by international organizations. It is, finally, the responsibility of the ordinary people and the non-governmental organizations in each country to put pressure on governments to see this is done. Alertness, awareness and action on the part of the citizens of each country thus are prerequisites (and the only guarantee) that UN resolutions will become reality.

Alternative development for North and South

As we already noted in Chapter 2, development policies implemented in past decades, firstly in the industrialized countries and more recently in many so-called developing countries, have proved to be very problematic for women. Already the move away from subsistence economy to monetary economy may have the effect of reducing their relative status and power. In traditional cultures women often have significant status due to their vital contribution to daily life — which is essential for the well-being of their families. And giving birth to children is another factor which traditionally has always conferred status. This change, and its consequences, are also described in the report of the International Workshop held in Bangkok in 1979:[3]

"The women's movement in the West passed through a period of intense, dramatic social and economic change that removed production from the home, contributed to devaluation of women's household production and household maintenance, their exclusion from social and economic power and resources, and the notion that men work and women have babies. Currently, women in the Third World are going through much the same trauma for many of the same reasons, though the direct economic and political forces are different. If women from capitalist and socialist countries, elite and poor, North and South, are to bridge the political and economic gulfs between them, the recognition of this fundamental commonality of economic processes is crucial."

A UNITAR report, *Women and Technology in the Industrialized Countries,* published in 1979,[4] analyses the problems created for women through technological development in the industrialized countries. The transfer of technology to developing countries in recent years has often completely failed. One common problem has been that most of the technological improvements come into the hands and the work of men, thus exacerbating the inequalities between men and women. Women remain in the traditional sector and work with old, inefficient tools, and are then accused of being old-fashioned and unproductive.

The ISIS report mentioned earlier criticizes international policies for their reluctance to see the links between development in the North and that in the South. They choose to see development as a far-distant affair and therefore, as the report says bluntly, "all the development strategies in the past, as well as the ones proposed for the future, lack validity ... Equality cannot be achieved as long as women are seen as marginal to the existence of men, society and development" in both developed and developing countries.

The NGO Conference on *Women and the New International Economic Order,* held in The Netherlands in 1982, went one step further and stated:

"Now we need another development both in the North and the South. Therefore, we need to recognize the views and interests of women and to create opportunities for their full participation at all levels of the society. Then the development would not any more take place only on economic terms, but also on human terms."

Awareness of the commonality of experiences of women in South and North is slowly expanding. Efforts to provide fora for the dialogue between South and North are springing up here and there. In addition to the few reports mentioned above, a major contribution to this dialogue was the International Women's Movement's anthology *Sisterhood is Global,* edited by Robin Morgan and published in 1984.[5] It is the broadest anthology so far on the subject, consisting of essays by women of more than 70 countries, 44 of them from the South, and demonstrates clearly how much women have in common, irrespective of stages of development, culture, language etc. The need is to be able to realize this, and what women can learn from each other's experiences in time and space. This awareness is the best basis for universal sisterhood, or solidarity between the women of the world.

A developmental analysis is to be found in the INSTRAW publication *Women in the World Economy.* This study takes a long-term view of economic changes, emphasizing trends in patterns of female employment since the 1960s. One of its conclusions — that international factors have contributed to the rise in female paid employment and influenced the structure of work opportunities in women's favour — should not be applied to the present situation without qualification. The book also evaluates the long-term sweep of events up to the 1980s, and concludes with a number of research findings that lead to policy recommendations that could have far-reaching implications for governments and private and public enterprises, as well as for international corporations and organizations.[6]

Within the public campaign of the Council of Europe in the first half of 1988 on North-South Interdependence and Solidarity, a symposium was held in Barcelona in May on *Women's Voice in the North-South Dialogue: Strategies for Interdependence and Solidarity.* It was an indication of slowly-growing awareness of the need both for a dialogue between South and North and to listen to the voices of women on both sides of the dialogue. Organized at the last moment, just before the ending of the campaign, it was the only meeting among the thirteen round-tables and symposia of the campaign to be specifically focused upon women.

Similar events have been organized at national level. The Finnish Equality Council organized a seminar on *Women and South-North Relations* in February 1988 in Helsinki, at which Dr. Krishna Patel of INSTRAW spoke on "The relevant development options from the point of view of women" and the voice of Southern women was heard in contributions from several developing country students. One of the authors of this book (Pietilä) introduced the topic "Crisis in the world economy — the policy of adjustment hits women", maintaining that the main problem of the South actually consists of the policies and practices of countries in the North.[7]

At the *Nordic Women's Forum* in Oslo, in the summer of 1988, the dialogue between women of North and South came into the picture in various ways. Many Nordic organizations had invited their sister groups in developing countries to send their representatives to the Forum, while Southern refugee and migrant women in the North came together in at least nine different national groupings. Development cooperation with the South and the New International Economic Order were discussed in a number of sessions. The Finns organized at this meeting a seminar on Women and North-South relations similar to that which had taken place in Helsinki, and an authentic voice of the South, the eloquent Kamla Bhasin from India, was one of the invited keynote speakers of the conference.

Notes

[1] Ingrid Palmer, *Recommendations relating to women and development emerging from conferences held under the auspices of the United Nations or the Specialized Agencies.* A/CONF.94/19, World Conference on the UN Decade for Women, Copenhagen, 1980.

[2] *Women in Development: A Resource Guide for Organization and Action.* Women's International Information and Communications Service (ISIS), Geneva, 1983.

[3] *Developing Strategies for the Future : Feminist Perspectives. op. cit.*

[4] Maria Bergson-Larsson, *Women and Technology in the Industrialized Countries.* UNITAR, United Nations, 1979.

[5] Robin Morgan, ed., *Sisterhood is Global.* The International Women's Movement Anthology, Anchor Press/Doubleday, New York, 1984.

[6] *Women in the World Economy.* An INSTRAW study edited by Susan Joekes, Oxford University Press, New York, 1986.

[7] *Women and North-South Relations.* Report of the Seminar in Helsinki, 19-20 February 1988. Ministry of Social Affairs and Health, Finland. Equality Publications, Series C, Working Papers 4/1988.

6.
An Institutional Breakthrough in the United Nations System

We referred, at the beginning of this study, to the very slow growth in the scope and importance of women's issues within the UN System. Until the beginning of the 1970's it was only marginal in comparison with the mainstream of UN activities. We also saw that during the 1970's the whole picture changed. From being only an issue of equality and human rights, the concern of women was finally recognized within the UN Decade for Women as being a central development issue. This was already a decisive change in attitudes and approaches towards women within the UN System.

But after the Nairobi Conference in 1985 the UN System really started to move *vis-à-vis* women's issues and concerns. There is reason to say that an actual breakthrough has taken place, one which is seen especially in the quality of approach to these issues. Now there is clearly a firm and definitive aspect to action concerning women: recognition of women, attention to women's interests and aspirations, and participation of women are, wherever possible, interwoven into the UN fabric in many different ways.

Why has this definitive approach finally come about? It is certainly due, at least in part, to the fact that the Forward-Looking Strategies were adopted unanimously in Nairobi: their obligations upon governments are as strong as it is possible to be within the UN System. This has given UN Secretariat units and organs concerned with the advancement of women a firm basis upon which to plan and undertake programmes for the implementation of the FLS. And they have actively used it, understanding that it is the will of the governments to go ahead.

Another factor behind this progress is the effect of the whole UN Decade for Women, which implied a constant process whereby women's issues were further studied. Extensive data were collected worldwide, and countless resolutions were passed in various UN bodies and organizations. Material produced for and adopted by the three World Conferences within the Decade convincingly demonstrate the importance of women's participation and their contribution towards dealing with the chores of humanity, today and in the future. Women have at last become literally visible within the UN System, and there would seem to be no looking back.

The impact of the international women's movement, of NGO action and women's research are factors behind this progress within the inter-governmental system. The process has without doubt been reciprocal. Women's research has gained ground rapidly in the last 10-15 years throughout the world, including in the Third World. Thus the women's movement has also been able to strengthen its base with the extensive outcome of research, and has gained in credibility and strength of argument. On the other hand, the NGO Forum held in parallel with each of the UN Conferences, and other international women's gatherings, have provided ample opportunities for the women's movement to share experiences, extend international networks and use these meetings as giant empowerment exercises, one after another.

This has produced growing pressure within UN member states, upon governments and officials in general and especially upon those in charge of UN affairs, and this is reflected in the increased activity and more positive stands taken by governments at UN meetings. Considering the many programmes and processes already in progress within the UN System with regard to the advancement of women and implementation of the FLS, it almost looks as though the United Nations is, for once, ahead of its member states and giving the lead as to how to proceed systematically in these issues. So reciprocal support by the women's movement and NGOs is still constantly needed in every country, to monitor government implementation of what they have agreed to in international fora.

Intergovernmental decision-making bodies
on women's issues

There are several intergovernmental organs and bodies in
the UN System concerned with decision-making and implementation of programmes and policies regarding the advancement of women. Decision-making and policy planning
take place first of all in the Commission on the Status of
Women, the Economic and Social Council (ECOSOC), and
in the General Assembly.

— The *Commission on the Status of Women* is the intergovernmental body which has the primary responsibility of dealing with issues concerning women and discussing them in
substance within the UN System. It is one of six functional
commissions of ECOSOC, to which it also presents its views
and recommendations. A resolution before the 1989 UN
General Assembly increased the number of member countries on the Commission from 32 to 45, of which one-third
will be replaced by new members every year. It was decided
in 1987 that the Commission would meet annually (instead
of biennially) until the year 2000, in order to monitor effectively the implementation of the FLS. Representatives of
NGOs in consultative status with ECOSOC are entitled to participate as observers in the sessions of the Commission.

— The *Economic and Social Council* (ECOSOC) is one of the
principal organs of the United Nations. As its name indicates, it coordinates all the economic and social activities of
the United Nations and the specialized agencies and institutions — known collectively as the United Nations family.
The Council has 54 members who serve for three years, 18
being elected each year to replace those whose term has
expired. From women's point of view ECOSOC is the most
important of the principal organs, since it receives the
reports and recommendations of the Commission on the
Status of Women, decides on them, and brings them
forward to the General Assembly for final confirmation.

— The *General Assembly* is the highest decision-making organ of the United Nations, in which all member governments are represented. It works through seven main committees. Most of the issues initiated by the Commission on
the Status of Women are discussed and decided upon in the

Third (Social, Humanitarian and Cultural) and Second (Economic and Financial) Committees. Since all member states participate in the resolutions of the General Assembly they also have the obligation to implement its decisions, especially if they are taken by consensus (unopposed); the obligatory effect is quite strong, even though General Assembly resolutions formally are only recommendations. Therefore it is important that proposals by the Commission on the Status of Women are finally adopted in the General Assembly.

The United Nations proper, as the central organ of the UN System or UN family of organizations, has also the role of co-ordinating the activities of the whole System, even though the Specialized Agencies are independent intergovernmental organizations in themselves. A very important body for this function is the *Administrative Committee on Coordination* (ACC), which the UN Secretary-General himself chairs and in which the executive heads of all the Agencies participate. Through this body important plans and programmes have obliged each of the Agencies to take its share of the implementation of the FLS, and to monitor its own activities in this respect.

Follow-up measures regarding policies and programmes on women

Measures for UN System implementation of the Nairobi FLS fall into three categories:
(a) improving the System-wide procedures for monitoring the implementation of the Forward-looking Strategies;
(b) programme coordination and integration of the Strategies into the policies and projects of the System;
(c) strengthening the role of national machinery for the advancement of women vis-à-vis the promotion, monitoring and implementation of the Strategies;
(d) establishment or strengthening of the focal points for the advancement of women. (A focal point is an organizational unit designed as a contact point both for external and internal communications concerning the advancement of women. It may consist of an individual member of the staff, a unit, division or department. There are altogether more

than 70 such focal points in the organizational units of the UN System).

The UN System has already made clear commitments and plans with regard to, on the one hand, making implementation of the Nairobi Strategies an integral, unquestionable part of the activities of all organs of the System; and, on the other hand, ensuring the monitoring and control of this process. A third basic requirement is to monitor, assess and evaluate global development from women's point of view as a continuous process, in order to keep track of the evolution of world development as seen with women's eyes.

The main measures and instruments for the realization of these aims in practice are the following:

— regular updating of the *World Survey on the Role of Women in Development* every five years; the first update after the Nairobi Conference was presented to the General Assembly in 1989;

— the *System-wide medium-term plan* for women and development for the period 1990-1995, already adopted by ECOSOC in 1987 in order to integrate the aims and strategies of the FLS into the general medium-term plans of the UN and all its agencies and organs;

— a *biennial, System-wide, monitoring* of progress made in implementing the Strategies (a continuing process of gathering and presenting information on the situation of women), including cross-organizational programme analysis within the UN System;

— a *five-year cycle of longer-term review and appraisal* (an evaluation of progress made in achieving the goals and objectives of the Strategies based primarily on the monitoring exercise).

Both monitoring and review and appraisal are to be executed at the national, regional and global levels, and reports presented to and studied by the Commission on the Status of Women, as the organ with main responsibility in these fields. In various UN documents concerning these plans there is clearly a serious attempt to make this process as effective as possible, and thus to ensure that the Forward-looking Strategies will make an impact. The wording of the documents indicates that a new approach has already been adopted by those in charge of preparations in the Secretariat.

They speak of "bringing the interests and needs of women into the mainstream of their organizations" instead of just speaking of the integration of women into development as such. They also call for "a simple, concise and direct form of reporting" and identification of "a clear and relevant set of statistical and other measurable indicators" in order to improve past UN practices in reporting and evaluating development.

Institutional structures within the UN System

The United Nations Secretariat is the executing body with the task of preparing the work of the intergovernmental bodies of the System, implementing the decisions approved by these bodies, and following up and facilitating the implementation of the decisions also in the member states. The primary institutional organs for the issues of special concern to women are different in character, and found in different parts of the organizational structure of the UN System.

The Division for the Advancement of Women is a particular organ within the Secretariat itself at the UN Office in Vienna. The Committee for the Elimination of Discrimination Against Women (CEDAW) is a particular juridical body monitoring the progress made in the implementation of the Convention on the Elimination of all forms of Discrimination against Women. The United Nations International Research and Training Institute for the Advancement of Women (INSTRAW) is an autonomous institute within the UN System and is located in Santo Domingo, Dominican Republic. And the central UN development agency, the United Nations Development Programme (UNDP), carries its part of the responsibility through its own Division for Women and Development and through the UN Development Fund for Women (UNIFEM).

The Division for the Advancement of Women

For thirty years, until 1975, the UN managed to function with only one small secretariat to deal with issues concerning women: the Branch for the Advancement of Women within the Centre for Social Development and Humanitarian Affairs (CSDHA). The Centre is part of the Department of International Economic and Social Affairs (DIESA), one of the major Departments of the organization, and is located now at the UN Office in Vienna. ECOSOC decided in spring 1988 that the status of the Branch would be elevated to that of a Division, which unfortunately did not imply any increase in staff and other resources.

The Division for the Advancement of Women is the central unit within the UN for all matters concerning women — an enormous task. It is the unit which prepares the drafts for all new plans and proated programmes, acts as the secretariat for the Commission on the Status of Women, follows up implementation of resolutions concerning women, acts as information source and contact point for the national machineries for the advancement of women in member states, etc. In principle, the Division covers the whole field, from the Convention on the Elimination of All Forms of Discrimination against Women to all aspects of the implementation of the Nairobi Forward-Looking Strategies.

The Committee on the Elimination of Discrimination against Women

This Committee (CEDAW) is a legal body stipulated by the Convention on the Elimination of All Forms of Discrimination against Women. It consists of 23 expert members appointed by governments but serving in their personal capacities. Its task is to supervise the implementation of the Convention, and governments are obliged to submit periodic reports to it. CEDAW has even the power to subject governments, one by one, to public scrutiny. Each government must submit its initial report within one year after the entry into force of the Convention in the country concerned, and then at least once every four years. The Committee may request additional or specific reporting whenever this appears necessary.

CEDAW meets once a year, alternatively in Vienna and New York, and international NGOs are entitled to send observers to the meetings. There is also an international network of activists and scholars, the International Women's

Rights Action Watch (IWRAW), which facilitates and monitors efforts to comply with the Convention.[1]

The United Nations International Research and Training Institute for the Advancement of Women

INSTRAW is an autonomous institution within the UN System, focusing entirely on women. Its origin stems from the World Conference on International Women's Year, 1975, in Mexico, where the need to establish a research and training institute for women was expressed. It took some time to establish the Institute, and it was not until 1982 that the actual work was begun. In 1983 INSTRAW settled into permanent premises in Santo Domingo, in the Dominican Republic. The formative process was concluded in early 1985 when the Institute's statute was endorsed by the United Nations General Assembly. The main tasks of the Institute are:

— to undertake research and provide training to integrate and mobilize women in the development process, to raise awareness and assist women to meet new challenges and directions;

— to act as a catalyst in the promotion of the role of women and the full participation of women in all aspects of the development process.

The guiding principle of INSTRAW's activities is to contribute to the changes in mainstream development which would fully value women's actual and potential contribution as an important development asset. Most of the Institute's programmes are implemented through co-operative arrangements with United Nations bodies, Specialized Agencies and Regional Commissions, as well as with governmental and non-governmental bodies, women's organizations and academic institutions. It has made some significant breakthroughs in the areas of statistics and indicators on women, policy design on women and development, and training and evaluation methodologies.

INSTRAW is funded solely from voluntary contributions from member states, intergovernmental and non-governmental organizations, foundations and private sources. In

1988 total contributions were approximately $1,100,000, contributed by both developed and developing countries.

The United Nations Development Fund for Women

In International Women's Year, 1975, a proposal was made to establish a Fund to assist women's development initiatives. It was officially established in 1976 as the Voluntary Fund for the UN Decade for Women, and in 1984 it became a permanent, autonomous United Nations Development Fund for Women, UNIFEM, associated with the UN Development Programme. UNIFEM focuses on development, and has two primary objectives:
— to provide direct financial and technical support to women involved in co-operative activities, food production, fuel and water supply, health services, small businesses, management and planning;
— to ensure that the needs of both women and men receive consideration when large-scale assistance is given to developing countries — through involvement in programming and project design, monitoring and evaluation.

UNIFEM is also financed by designated, voluntary contributions from governments, organizations and individuals. In 1988 contributions reached $8 million, Canada and Norway being the largest donors. Since becoming operational in 1978 UNIFEM has supported nearly 400 activities for women in over 100 developing countries. Yet the Fund can respond to less than half of the deserving appeals it receives for assistance.

The UNDP's Division for Women in Development

Among the 67 focal points on women within the UN System, the United Nations Development Programme's Division for Women in Development is a very special one. It is probably the earliest, if we count the work of a UNDP principal officer on Women in Development, Ulla Olin, long before the IWY.[2] It was extended amd strengthened to a Division in 1987 as part of the growing attention being given to Women in Development in the work of UNDP. Its main functions are:

— to co-operate with operational units of UNDP in the identification of women's roles in the economic and social development of countries receiving aid, and ensure that these roles are reflected in programming;

— to liaise with the focal points for the promotion of women as project participants and beneficiaries established in UNDP country offices and headquarters units;

— to work closely with the UN Development Fund for Women (UNIFEM) to ensure complementarity and harmonization of approaches;

— to develop guidelines and training programmes on women and development for UNDP staff and interested governments;

— to develop and monitor the implementation of guidelines for the recruitment and advancement of women in UNDP's administration, and to ensure an increase in the proportion of women within UNDP and in the organization's senior posts.

One result of UNDP's early engagement was the publication of a guide booklet on Women in Development in 1975.[3] In 1986 UNDP produced a comprehensive and systematic *Programme Advisory Note on Women in Development,*[4] prepared in collaboration with 13 Specialized Agencies and provided for their use in practical execution of UNDP-supported projects in the field.

Notes

[1] *The Women's Watch,* quarterly newsletter, International Women's Rights Action Watch/WPPD, Humphrey Institute of Public Affairs, 301 19th Ave. South, Minneapolis, Min. 55455, USA.

[2] As one outcome of Ulla Olin's work we have already, in Chapter 2, cited UNDP's inter-organizational assessment on Women and Development (see Note No. 4).

[3] Esther Boserup and Christina Liljencrantz, *Integration of Women in Development — Why, When, How?* UNDP New York, 1975.

[4] *Women in Development,* UNDP Programme Advisory Note, Programme Policy and Evaluation, Technical Advisory Division, UNDP New York, May 1986.

7.
The UN System's
Concrete Commitment to Women

The System-wide Plan for Women
and Development, 1990-1995

The most impressive commitment of the UN System to the realization of the Nairobi Strategies is, however, the System-wide Medium-term Plan for Women and Development. The FLS document contains a request to the Secretary-General to initiate such a plan, and in the autumn of 1985 ECOSOC requested the Secretary-General, in his capacity as chairman of the Administrative Committee on Coordination (ACC — see previous chapter), to prepare a comprehensive medium-term plan. The point of departure is stated in the Introduction to the Plan:

> "The formulation of the Forward-looking Strategies and their adoption by consensus were a major landmark in the advancement of women internationally, and a significant achievement for multilateralism. In adopting the Strategies, 157 States joined in making a commitment to take concrete measures by the year 2000 to eliminate all forms of sex-based discrimination.
> "Strategies must be translated by each of those concerned into concrete tasks if the objectives are to be achieved. The tasks envisaged cut across the traditional sectoral lines along which the work of the UN System is organized."

These are actually very hard requirements for the UN System, which over the decades has become famous for its 'compartmentalization'. The implementation of the Nairobi

Strategies is thus prompting the restructuring and stream-lining process of the System — needs which have also been indicated for other reasons.

The System-wide Medium-term Plan for Women and Development, 1990-1995, was adopted in the second regular session of ECOSOC in the summer of 1987.[1] It is a Plan based on the FLS and is intended to translate the development aspects of the FLS into a consistent and efficient approach to guide the planning and programming of individual organizations of the UN System. Its timing is appropriate for facilitating the preparations of the medium-term plans for 1992-1997 of the UN proper and the Specialized Agencies.

The System-wide Plan is also based upon the various programmes and plans already adopted in several UN organizations, and particularly in the special World Conferences during the 1970's and the beginning of the 1980's (see Annex 4; the ways in which women's interests and perspectives were handled in these conferences have been discussed in chapter 5). It seeks to integrate activities not only with regard to development but also directed towards equality and peace, since they are both preconditions and goals of development. The Plan is composed of 23 sub-programmes, organized into six programme areas:

1. *Elimination of legal and attitudinal forms of discrimination:* international standards; promoting more positive attitudes towards the role of women in development.

2. *Access to productive resources, income and employment:* trends and policies in women's employment; vocational training; food and agriculture; industry; entrepreneurship and access to credit; informal sector.

3. *Access to services:* health, nutrition and family planning; literacy and education; housing, settlement, water, energy and transport; other social infrastructure and support services.

4. *Decision-making:* participation in management and decision-making; participation in groups, associations, co-operatives, trade unions and other non-governmental organizations.

5. *Improving means of international action:* development of statistics and indicators; information dissemination; research, policy analysis and dissemination; technical co-operation, training and advisory services.

6.   *Comprehensive approaches* to women and development: analysis of the interrelationship of factors affecting women and development; monitoring and review and appraisal of basic policy guidelines and national experiences; strengthening national machineries and mechanisms for planning and policy-making; coordinating a System-wide approach to women and development.

The System-wide Medium-term Plan is intended to provide a framework to guide individual organizations in the framing of their own plans and programmes on women and development during the period 1990-1995. It is intended to be a basis for information exchange and co-operation among organizations, and for determining the areas in which joint action will be required, with implementation to take place within the individual programmes of the organizations concerned.

As one can see, the Plan covers a wide range of activities — as do the Forward-looking Strategies. Therefore it involves the whole UN System too. It is impossible to summarize it, we can only try to highlight a few especially interesting and innovative aspects of it. Even the attempt to select particularly important aspects is inevitably a very individual choice as to what is important.

Each sub-programme is structured to indicate first the inter-governmental objectives, then the UN System objectives, and finally the strategy for achieving the objectives.

Towards a coherent policy

It is obvious that many of the obstacles to women's full participation in development are interrelated. They have to be examined from a historical, multi-dimensional and cross-sectoral perspective so that coherent policy measures can be developed to overcome them. The System-wide Plan is intended to develop this kind of comprehensive approach. As designed, it seeks:
— to analyse the interrelationship of factors affecting women and development;
— to monitor, review and appraise the basic policy guidelines on women and development;

— to strengthen national machineries and mechanisms for planning and policy-making;

— to coordinate a System-wide approach to women and development.

There is a natural connection also between the System-wide Plan and the Convention on the Elimination of All Forms of Discrimination against Women. Information is to be gathered globally and regionally on national policies and experience for the monitoring at the same time of the implementation of both the Forward-looking Strategies and the Convention.

Possibilities for the UN System to succeed in really high-quality analysis of the interrelationships between various factors related to the advancement of women, and monitoring and reviewing progress made, depend decisively on national and regional research and planning capabilities. If national statistical and research institutions are not capable of providing adequate data, the UN System cannot produce accurate and reliable reviews with regard to the global situation. Therefore there is a special programme in the System-wide Plan:

(a) to develop statistics and indicators on women and development;

(b) to improve public information and information networks in this field;

(c) to improve the quality of information and policy analysis on women and development, and the dissemination of educational materials in this field;

(d) to improve the procedures for designing and implementing technical co-operation;

(e) to improve the participation of women in science and technology for development, and to ensure that scientific and technological progress benefits women as well as men.

Reliable, comprehensive and unbiased statistics and indicators are prerequisites for mapping the world situation and progress made from the point of view of women. Here the International Research and Training Institute for the Advancement of Women (INSTRAW) has a very important role. All the work in this field is carried out within the conceptual and organizational frameworks developed by the UN

System and is periodically reviewed by the Statistical Commission of the United Nations.

Women's research and public information

In the System-wide Plan there is quite a strong emphasis on public information. Information and education are very much relied upon in the elimination of legal and attitudinal forms of discrimination (Programme 1). The importance of mass media and journalists — particularly women journalists — is well recognized. Mass media should present a correct picture of the quantity, quality and importance of women's contributions to the life and well-being of their fellow-citizens everywhere. There are training programmes, fellowships and internships planned for women journalists to familiarize themselves with facts concerning women's lives and contributions which have been given all too little attention in mass media in the past. These efforts should not, however, be directed only to women journalists: their male colleagues need even more to have their eyes opened.

Women's Studies are seen as another important means of information and education for women themselves. The objective is to promote women's studies in the curricula of schools, colleges and universities in all member countries. The UN System is ready to help developing countries establish such programmes by providing advisory services, guidelines on content and curricula, and grants and training services.

As a particular input into women's studies and public information, a reference guide on the history of women and development worldwide, based on existing studies and the commissioning of new ones in areas not previously covered, is planned for completion within the forthcoming five-year period.

The Plan seems to be aware of the risk of overemphasizing the economic and material components of development — as has been very much the case in Western civilizations for decades. In connection with the promotion of more positive attitudes towards the role of women in development, attention is also given to the traditional role played by women in the family and community in maintaining and transmitting the values, traditional knowledge and know-how that form part of cultural heritage and identity. Women's contribution to the renewal and enrichment of cultural identities — through cultural communication and creative work — will also be promoted.

The System-wide Medium-term Plan was intended to provide a framework to guide individual organizations in the framing of their own plans and programmes on women and development during the period 1990-1995 — a plan which would provide a basis for information exchange and co-operation among organizations. It would also serve as a basis for determining the areas in which joint action would be required, while implementation was to take place within the individual programmes of the organizations concerned.

In general, there seems to be much more emphasis in the System-wide Plan on activities and programmes aimed at conscientization of women themselves than there is in the Forward-looking Strategies.

Income and employment are not enough

Programmes 2 and 3, women's access to productive resources, income and employment, and access to services, are the most important chapters in the Plan. They cover the whole range of issues relating to working life, such as equality in employment and salaries, vocational training and training with regard to women and development issues, food and agriculture, industry, entrepreneurship and access to credit, and the multiplicity of the informal sector. And in Programme 3 there are basic services such as health, nutrition and family planning, literacy and education, housing, settlement, water, energy and transport, social infrastructure and support services.

All these issues are in many ways interrelated, and for the improvement of the practical conditions of life they are indeed decisive. In this connection there exists the same well-known problem: women are the ones who have always made, and continue to make, huge contributions in these fields, but their unpaid contribution remains largely unrecognized and uncounted. Thus development efforts seldom match the needs as seen by women themselves. The proposed measures have often implied increasing the workload of women instead of making it less burdensome. These trends need to be identified and rectified.

In the Plan the distribution of labour between men and women, especially in rural and traditional societies, needs to be further examined. It is well known that, in many countries, women's burden is constantly increasing, due in large part to environmental problems, carrying water and collecting fuel over ever longer distances being traditionally considered women's work. The Plan discusses the role of women from all possible angles; it should also touch upon the need to change the customary roles of men too, even though many problems for women stem from the reluctance of men to change their customs and behaviour.

In accordance with the Plan an interesting study on the effectiveness of international instruments is on the way in the field of women's employment. A comprehensive evaluation of the impact of international instruments (e.g. ILO Conventions) is planned for completion in 1993. It includes the question of women's access to employment and their working conditions, with particular emphasis on labour market transformations caused by technological development. The study will be published in 1995 and then made available to governments and workers' and employers' organizations for use in the formulation of national policies. A manual on equality of opportunity and treatment for men and women workers will also be produced.

In connection with plans for food and agriculture, it is proposed to reassess the basic goals of development in the light of rural women's contributions in food production, as well as in the home. The UN System will provide governments with adequate information regarding women's key roles in rural development which, if appropriately supported, can lead to the realization of basic development goals such as food security, reduction of rural poverty, decline of population growth and adequate nutrition.

Last but not least, the Plan comes to decision-making. It is emphasized strongly, both in the Nairobi Strategies and the World Survey, that the equitable participation of women in decision-making at all levels is a key issue concerning the influence of women in their societies. Without participation in decision-making there is little hope that women's interests and aspirations will be taken into consideration in their societies.

The System-wide Plan makes a strong link in this connection between development, equality and peace:

> "Women's participation in decision-making processes is fundamental to the achievement of the other objectives of the Plan. This programme emphasizes the means by which women can actively participate in decision-making, including political decisions, the determination of policies, the design of programmes, the allocation of resources, the implementation of activities and the assessment of results in all fields, including the promotion and maintenance of peace and security."

Nevertheless, the Plan speaks about women's participation in decision-making primarily only in quantitative terms; the more women in decision-making bodies, the better decisions! A quantitative approach does not necessarily guarantee that women's views and values are represented — a fact well known in, for example, Scandinavia where the proportion of women in parliaments has been fairly high for a long time. The crux of the matter is the level of awareness of women participating in decision-making. On that depends whether the increasing number of women in decision-making will make any difference or not.

Women's participation in groups, associations, co-operatives, trade unions and other non-governmental organizations is also discussed in the Plan. Trade unions and other organizations should seek to encourage women to become members. Instead of primarily addressing existing institutions to seek and encourage women, the Plan should also directly address women and encourage them to establish their own organizations and structures as they themselves find desirable and feasible. In women-only structures they could support each other, develop their own perspectives and formulate their aims and aspirations. Both are needed: opportunities for women to meet and act among themselves, and organizations in which women can participate together with men, express their views and be heard.

Needs in both North and South

No distinctions are made in the Plan as to whether the objectives are particularly directed to the developing or the so-called developed world. Many of the proposals are obviously relevant to any country, for example those concerning support services. The Plan sets as intergovernmental objectives:
— to develop social infrastructures for the care and education of children of working parents in order to reduce their double burden;
— to provide support services for care of the elderly and disabled;
— to encourage flexible working hours
— to help women become better-informed consumers
— to prevent and reduce family violence.

In this connection there seems to be a problem as to whether to indicate to whom the support services should be provided, when they concern women, men or both. Some indications even seem to be inverted. With regard to reducing the double burden, the text speaks about parents, although the double burden is usually on the mother. Then, consumer information is indicated only for women, as if men were better-informed consumers already.

The question of family violence — the different forms of violence against women and measures to deal with it — is as vague here as in the FLS. This appears to be a burning, universal problem for women with which the UN System seems to have difficulty coming to grip. Rape as gross violence against a woman's body and dignity is not yet mentioned in the documents at all.

Another System-wide Plan for 1996-2001

The System-wide Medium-term Plan for 1990-1995 is an almost unbelievable UN document. Never before has there been a plan which really covers the whole system of UN organs and agencies and gives them tasks to be implemented for a particular aim. As an annex to the Plan there is a worktable which distributes tasks to the various parts of the UN family in the field of women and development. (See Annex 3 to this book). The enormous amount of work required to prepare this worktable has been carried out by all these UN bodies through the Administrative Committee on Coordination (ACC).

The implementation of the System-wide Medium-term Plan for Women and Development is already well on the way. Although the Plan officially starts in 1990, the organizations that have agreed to implement the tasks addressed to them in the Plan reported already to ECOSOC in the summer of 1989 with regard to their programmes for fulfilling their obligations (document E/1989/16).

The System-wide Plan means, in practice, that the implementation of the Nairobi FLS is now built into the UN System, and that the United Nations family has accepted it as a joint commitment. One example of how this built-in procedure works is the ECOSOC request to the Secretary-General in the spring of 1988 that he "should identify the implementation of the Nairobi Forward-looking Strategies for the Advancement of Women, and the status of women in general, as a global priority in the introduction to the next medium-term plan (of the United Nations proper, 1992-1997)".

But medium-term plans usually cover only five years. Therefore work has already started with regard to a second System-wide Medium-term Plan for Women and Development for the period 1996 — 2001. In preparing this Plan the experiences of all agencies in implementation of the first Plan will be utilized, and all new trends appearing during those years will be taken into consideration. So the continuation of the process for implementing the Nairobi FLS has now been quite well secured within the UN System even beyond the year 2000 — so far the target of the FLS.

What else is needed to make the FLS a reality in these forthcoming years? This question will be tackled in the last chapter of this book.

Note

[1] International Co-operation and Coordination within the United Nations System. Proposed System-wide Medium-term plan for Women and Development for the period 1990-1995. Report of the ACC, E/1987/52, 7 April 1987.

8.
The Emerging Rights of Women

Inequality and discrimination, whether based on race, colour, culture, language, religion or sex, often take similar forms in practice. However, there are specific characteristics of discrimination against women which do not occur elsewhere. Sex attitudes, beliefs, prejudices and myths are much more deeply rooted in the basic structures of cultures and human behaviour than are many other customs, norms and traditions.

In the United Nations Charter...

A mandate to bring about equality between the sexes was already clear in the UN Charter, where "the Peoples of the United Nations determine to reaffirm faith in fundamental human rights, in the dignity and worth of the human person, in the equal rights of men and women..." In Article 1 of the Charter it is further stated that "the Purposes of the United Nations are ... to achieve international co-operation in promoting and encouraging respect for human rights and for fundamental freedoms for all without distinction as to race, sex, language or religion."

At the very first session of the UN General Assembly, a Commission was appointed to draft the *Universal Declaration of Human Rights*. One of the most outstanding women of the time, Eleanor Roosevelt, presided that Commission. When the Declaration was adopted in 1948 it contained the words: "All human beings are born free and equal in dignity and rights." The second Article is even more specific: "Everyone is entitled to all the rights and freedoms set forth in this Declaration, without distinction of any kind, such as race, colour, sex, language..."

Based on the principles of the Charter and the Universal Declaration of Human Rights, much work has been done to produce further, more binding, more concrete and precise provisions on equality of the sexes. Originally, this work took place mainly in the International Labour Organization, where the Conventions on Equal Remuneration for Work of Equal Value, and Discrimination in Respect of Employment and Occupation, were adopted in the 1950's. In the United Nations itself, during the 1940's and 1950's, women's issues were debated only in bodies specifically concerned with human rights.

The Commission on the Status of Women had, however, been established in 1946, with a mandate to study and prepare recommendations on human rights issues of special concern to women. At first, the creation of a commission specifically devoted to women's issues drew some criticism, but the work it has carried out over the years has amply demonstrated its importance. Had the questions of equality between the sexes and women's status been on the agenda only of the Commission on Human Rights — along with so many other issues — they would hardly have received the necessary attention.

The Commission on the Status of Women

The first task of the Commission on the Status of Women was to determine in which conditions and situations, all over the world, the most severe forms of discrimination against women occurred. Four fields, in particular, were found to give cause for concern:

— political rights and the possibility of exercising them;
— legal rights of women, both as individuals and as family members;
— access of girls and women to education and training, including vocational training;
— working life.

In recent decades recommendations and conventions have been prepared and adopted by the United Nations, Unesco and ILO in all four. Figure 2 lists some of the most significant of those relating specifically to women. Figure 3 (page 124) gives an idea of the many different stages by which an issue becomes the subject of a UN Convention and is then, finally, implemented at the national level.

The subjects and history of these Conventions are a sad reflection on the central problems of women which still remain as the 20th century draws to a close, and on the important attempts made by the United Nations to redress them. Political rights for women, for instance, were in force in only 30 of the 51 countries which signed the UN Charter in 1945. Within the 45 years of the UN's existence, partly prompted by the UN Convention on the Political Rights of Women, most countries have granted women the opportunity to participate in politics. By 1988, 94 countries had ratified the Convention and, in fact, countries where these rights still do not exist are rare.

Also pointedly evocative of the situation of women were the reasons which led to the adoption of the *Convention on Consent to Marriage, Minimum Age of Marriage and Registration of Marriages,* in 1962. At that time, in much of the world, women still had nothing to say in the choice of their marriage partners or the age at which their marriages took place; they were mere commodities in the hands of their parents and families, who had full power to decide upon their fate. In many countries women had no rights within marriage either; they could be abandoned at any time and thrown out of their homes and families. The provision regarding obligatory registration of marriages was, therefore, necessary in order that the rights of the wife be officially recognized.

Traffic in persons (women!)

Efforts to prevent prostitution and exploitation of women through procurement provide a good example of attempts to solve a concrete, practical problem by means of international conventions. Widespread attention has been focussed on this problem since the middle of the last century, when it was known as "sexual slavery". The women's movement and a number of non-governmental organizations had already made a proposal to the League of Nations about prohibition of sexual slavery, and a comprehensive document was drafted for adoption by the League which, unfortunately, did not pass through before the outbreak of World War II.

Figure 2: Selected Conventions of Concern to Women

Adopted		In Force	Ratification (as of end 1988)
1949	Convention for the Suppression of Traffic in Persons and the Exploitation of the Prostitution of others	1951	59
1951	Equal Remuneration for Men and Women Workers for Work of Equal Value (ILO No. 100)	1953	109
1952	Convention on the Political Rights of Women	1954	94
1958	Discrimination in Respect of Employment and Occupation (ILO No. 111)	1960	109
1960	International Convention against Discrimination in Education (Unesco)	1962	77
1962	Convention on Consent to Marriage, Minimum Age of Marriage, and Registration of Marriages	1964	35
1979	Convention on the Elimination of All Forms of Discrimination Against Women	1981	94
1981	Convention concerning Equal Opportunities and Equal Treatment for Men and Women Workers: Workers with Family Responsibilities (ILO No. 156)	1982	13

See also Annex 6: Relevant International Instruments.

The issue came up again in the United Nations soon after its foundation, and in 1949 the *Convention for the Suppression of the Traffic in Persons and the Exploitation of the Prostitution of Others* was adopted. It came into force in 1951 and, by 1988, had been ratified by 59 governments. The Convention commits signatories to the punishment of any person who procures or entices another into prostitution or who owns or manages a brothel, to the supervision of employment agencies with a view to preventing traffic in women, and to the provision of rehabilitation for the victims of prostitution.

However, although this Convention was adopted almost 40 years ago, it has still not been possible — either by national or international measures — to end even such clear and concrete practices as prostitution and the exploitation of others by prostitution. On the contrary, prostitution has become big business, and 'traffic in persons' has taken on new and more sophisticated forms and extended on an unforeseen scale to become an international trade, one of the latest forms of which is the procurement of submissive and adaptable wives from South-East Asia for Western men (Western women having become all too independent and demanding!). And massive expansion of intercontinental tourism, coupled with the deteriorating situation of women in many developing countries, has made sex holidays an ever more flourishing phenomenon.

If nothing else, however, the Convention does give international justification to attempts to spotlight these and other related problems (such as sexual harassment and exploitation of women workers in transnational corporations in developing countries), and like all other intergovernmental conventions provides a strong, legitimate basis for people to put pressure on governments to take adequate remedial measures.

What does 'status' mean?

During the course of its work the UN Commission on the Status of Women has also questioned what the concept of 'status' actually means. Status in relation to what? How can status be measured? What is the yardstick? Usually the status of women is compared with that of men in terms of working life, education, access to services and benefits, and opportunities to participate in decision-making and politics.

These questions became especially relevant at the end of the 1960's and the beginning of the 1970's, when growing interest was focused on the interrelationships between family planning and the status of women. The issues of family planning and birth control came into UN discussions in connection with debates on population growth which, particularly in the 1960's, was considered one of the major problems of developing countries. In 1965 the Commission on the Status of Women requested the UN Secretary-General to provide it "... with a report on the effect of the lack of family planning on the status of women ... and the relation between family planning and the status of women".

Following the declaration of 1974 as World Population Year, and 1975 as International Women's Year, the importance of the links between family planning and the status of women loomed even larger. Studies on the world's population problems and the factors influencing them revealed more and more the key position of women in birth control and limitation of population growth. At the same time, in preparations for IWY, the right of and possibility for women to control the number and spacing of their children emerged as an issue of decisive importance to the status of women and to all aspects of their lives.

It is evident that the status of women cannot here be defined merely by comparison with the status of men. The crux of the issue is whether a woman has the right and the means to control what happens to her own body. From time immemorial women have, in this respect, been at the mercy of men, prevailing cultural traditions and nature. Giving birth, breast-feeding and nurturing children has always put very definite limits to whatever else a woman could, or would like to, do with her life.

In response to the request of the Commission, the UN Secretary-General appointed a Special Rapporteur for a study on the interrelationship between the status of women and family planning.[1] The report, dated 27 November 1973, discusses the concept of 'the status of women' rather thoroughly, and attempts to define and pinpoint it more clearly than in the past:

"Status usually refers to the position or positions a person or group holds in the structure of a society — in its educational institution, its occupational structure, its political system, in the family, and so on. To these various positions — a number of which may be occupied by a single individual simultaneously in his or her capacity as a member of several social groups — are ascribed varying degrees of power, privilege and prestige. Thus, the concept of status implies a hierarchical arrangement of positions. Each position also involves a set of rights and obligations which the occupant is expected to fulfill.

"When we speak of the 'status of women', then, we are speaking of the conjunction of positions a woman occupies at any one point in time, as a worker, student, wife, mother, church member, political worker, or whatever, and of the rights and duties she is expected to exercise in her active role as occupant of these positions. It is generally accepted that women are discriminated against, and that men have more prestige, power and privileges in almost all societies. But the direct measurement of status is a difficult and complex problem which hinders investigations of the causes and consequences of this particular form of stratification."

One of the difficulties was to produce a cross-culturally valid definition of the status of women. Such statistical indicators as life expectancy, years of formal schooling, labour force participation rates, etc. do not always reveal the actual conditions of women in all societies. No internationally-comparable social indicators were available.

"After all, status is not a fixed, rigid concept but one that changes over time. Not only do women occupy different positions in the social structure as they pass through the life cycle, but the very bases upon which the community ascribes power, privilege and prestige may also change. The difficulties here are compounded by the fact that the definition itself of what constitutes 'high' or 'low' status depends on the perspective of the observer.

"How does one deal, for example, with the situation in which a woman's prestige in the eyes of her family and her community rises with every child she bears, or a man is ashamed when his wife takes work outside the home? The 'objective' researcher may define the first woman's 'status' as low and the second's as higher, in direct contradiction of the norms of the woman's own social situation."

The report seeks a definition which would be as culture-free as possible and enable the differentiation of the status of women from that of men in a given society. It concludes that the best method to date is to assess the status of an individual high or low according to the actual control that he/she has over his/her own life.

"To what extent do women as compared to men have access to knowledge, to economic resources, to political power, and what degree of personal autonomy do these resources permit? A related and more quantifiable approach is to assess the range of choices or options available to women as compared to men in the same society (or to women in different societies or subgroups) in the areas of education, employment, political life, family life and other relevant areas. Both approaches are based on the assumption that low status derives from a lack of control over material or social resources and a lack of choice in the unfolding of one's destiny."

A new human right

The fact that a study on family planning from the point of view of women necessitated a redefinition of the whole concept of 'status' indicates how very crucial this question is to women. However, the subject would hardly have received the attention it deserves, even at this late day and age, had not the problems created by rapid population growth in developing countries brought it into the limelight.

By the end of the 1960's, access to family planning was beginning to be recognized as a new basic human right, which also indicates the growing importance of the issue. It was mentioned for the first time in this form in the *Declara-*

tion of Teheran, which resulted from the International Conference on Human Rights in 1968, and the following year was included in the *Declaration on Social Progress and Development* by the UN General Assembly. More recently, it has been incorporated into several resolutions and documents, such as the *World Population Plan of Action* (1974) and the *Declaration of Mexico and Plan of Action of the IWY* (1975).[2] It is included, as an obligatory provision, in the *Convention on the Elimination of All Forms of Discrimination against Women*[3] (1979), where it is stipulated:

"States Parties shall take all appropriate measures to eliminate discrimination against women in all matters relating to marriage and family relations and in particular shall ensure, on a basis of equality of men and women ...

"... the same rights to decide freely and responsibly on the number and spacing of their children and to have access to the information, education and means to enable them to exercise these rights."

The recognition of the right to family planning and access to the information and practical means necessary to exercise this right is a historic step, frequently cited as the single most important factor in recent years in the improvement of the status of women. With this right as a practical, everyday asset women the world over have moved into a new age: one in which they may eventually have the right to control their own lives.

The ability to choose how many children they will have, and to space their births appropriately, also provides women with the opportunity to exercise other human rights more fully than before. Firstly, they will be able to plan and organize their lives in such a way as to obtain education and training; better education will enhance their economic independence and, hence, their participation in the cultural and political lives of their countries. Family planning also helps families to plan and improve their living standards, so that they will be able to provide better conditions, education and health care to those children they choose to have.

Along with the right to family planning, another basic human right becomes a reality: the right to be born a wanted child. The most felicitous start possible to one's life, this may have far more meaning than has ever been realized. And it is one right for which those principally concerned will never have been able themselves to fight!

The Convention on the Elimination of All Forms of Discrimination Against Women

By far the most important of the conventions on the status of women is the *Convention on the Elimination of All Forms of Discrimination against Women*, which was adopted in 1979 and entered into force in 1981 following ratification by the required 20 countries. It is a concise and comprehensive conclusion to the long process which has taken place within the UN System to incorporate the principles of women's rights and equality between the sexes in the provisions of international law. It includes, in their most precise form, all provisions aiming at the elimination of discrimination against women previously covered by separate conventions. It also contains provisions covering issues omitted from earlier conventions. The different stages in this process are listed in Figure 3.

The Convention (the full text of which is given in Annex 1) also provides for follow-up, obliging member states to report to the UN Committee on the Elimination of Discrimination against Women (CEDAW) on legislative and other steps taken to implement its provisions. A government must first report to the Committee one year after the Convention has entered into force in its country, and every four years thereafter. CEDAW is composed of 23 elected experts nominated by the States parties to the Convention.

The case of Finland again provides an example of how the Convention works in practice. The Finnish Government signed it in 1980 at the World Conference of the UN Decade for Women in Copenhagen, along with many other governments. However, it took several years before Finland was able to ratify the Convention because certain aspects of national legislation did not conform with it. Following its adoption by the UN, and the Finnish Government's signature thereto, several Finnish organizations and activists were

Figure 3: Year by Year Progress of the Convention on the Elimination of All Forms of Discrimination Against Women

1945   United Nations Charter reaffirms "faith in fundamental human rights ... in the equal rights of men and women ..." (Preamble).

1947   The Commission on the Status of Women is established, to initiate and monitor UN action on behalf of women.

1948   Universal Declaration of Human Rights proclaims "every- one is entitled to all the rights and freedoms set forth in this Declaration without distinction of any kind, such as race, colour, sex ..." (Article 2).

1954   General Assembly recognizes that women are "subject to ancient laws, customs and practices" inconsistent with the Declaration and calls on governments to "abolish" them (Res. 843 (IX)).

1963   General Assembly, noting continued discrimination, calls for a draft on a Declaration on the Elimination of Discrimination Against Women (Res.1921 (XVII)).

1966   Commission submits draft to General Assembly which returns it for revision, "bearing in mind the amendments which have been submitted" (Res. 2199 (XX1)

1967   General Assembly adopts the revised Declaration "to ensure the universal recognition in law and in fact of the principle of equality of men and women" (Res.2263 (XXII)).

1968   Economic and Social Council initiates reporting system on implementation by governments of Declaration's provisions (ECOSOC Res. 1325 (XLIV)).

1970   General Assembly urges "the ratification of or accession to the relevant international instruments relating to the status of women" (Res.2716 (XXV).

1972   The UN Secretary-General asks the views of government on the "nature and content of a new instrument".

1973   ECOSOC appoints a 15-member working group to begin drafting a convention.

1975   International Women's Year World Plan of Action calls for "the preparation and adoption of the convention on the elimination of discrimination against women with effective procedures for its implementation" (Item 198).

1977   General Assembly appoints Working Group of the Whole "to continue consideration" of the draft (Res.32/136).

1978   General Assembly recommends the working group complete its task (Res.33/177).

1979   General Assembly adopts completed draft, inviting signatures and ratifications (Res.34/180).

1981   Convention on the Elimination of All Forms of Discrimination against Women enters into force with required 20 ratifications.

Source: *Rights of Women,* Workbook of the International Women's Tribune Center, New York, 1983.

able to use the Convention as a basis on which to argue for the necessary changes in the law, and a new law on equality for men and women was drafted.

Thanks to the Convention there was pressure on the Government from two sides: the Finnish people, organizations and groups and the National Equality Council from inside, and UN expectations from outside. Finnish pressure groups did not hesitate to argue that the international image of the Finnish Government would be tarnished if the necessary changes in the law were not enacted and the Convention ratified soon — at the very latest prior to the 1985 World Conference to Review and Appraise the Achievements of the UN Decade for Women. The names of countries which have ratified the Convention are presented in the UN General Assembly every year, and attract special attention among governments — as do those names which are missing.

Thus, international conventions and national legislation are ways of rectifying injustices and inequalities and may also, indirectly, bring about changes in attitudes. However, it often seems to be more difficult to change attitudes than to change laws. And the real changes will only take place when attitudes change.

Notes

[1] Helvi Sipilä, Study on the Interrelationship of the Status of Women and Family Planning. Report of the Special Rapporteur, E/CN.6/575, Add.1, 2 and 3, 27 November 1973.

[2] Declaration of Mexico and Plan of Action of the IWY, *op. cit.*

[3] *op. cit.*

9.

Promises and Doubts:
Women's Future with the United Nations

The bright picture ...

When we read about all the programmes and plans adopted so far and introduced in the previous chapters we may feel that everything is fine, that the UN can no longer escape recognition of the half of humanity "who bear more than half the sky on their shoulders". Member governments have given firm promises to rectify imbalances between men and women in the UN as well as in global and national development. Now the issue is the keeping of those promises — and for women to see to it that their governments implement what they have decided.

Documents such as the Nairobi Forward-looking Strategies, the World Survey on the Role of Women in Development and its first update, and the System-wide Medium-term Plan for Women and Development represent very advanced thinking in comparison with mainstream UN thinking. They represent radical new inclinations within the UN System. But there is hardly any glimpse yet of this kind of approach in documents and discussions dealing with, for example, disarmament and security issues, in UNCTAD and GATT, or even relating to environment issues. It will take time for these new perspectives to be recognized by the 'hard liners' among the UN institutions; System-wide plans do not penetrate automatically, by any means.

But, if we compare the above-mentioned documents with advanced feminist thinking on equality, development and peace, they are far behind in their visions and approaches. The most representative group for advanced feminist thinking is the DAWN group, introduced in Chapter 2: they have already gone far beyond formal, bureaucratic equality thinking, and challenge patriarchal, centralized, hierarchical development patterns as such. Their principal point of departure is that, due to women's authentic experiences in life, they have their own contribution to make towards the visions, values and patterns of development — a contribution quite different from that of men. Therefore it is essential that women's voice is heard equally with men's, and that they have equal opportunities to contribute to planning, design, decision-making and implementation of development in their countries.

Other chapters have contained many examples of how advanced feminist thinking has influenced the texts of the documents introduced. The concepts of Equality, Development and Peace developed considerably during the UN Decade for Women and beyond. The process goes on, the latest papers — like the System-wide Medium-term Plan — representing yet more advanced thinking than the FLS itself. And the updated World Survey on the Role of Women in Development is more clear-sighted and better structured than the first one.

Equality is no longer only a legitimate right of women, but an absolute social necessity to bring about more balanced and humane development in society. Full participation of women on their own terms is "a condition for achieving sustainable development", as stated at the beginning of the System-wide Plan. Equal participation and representation of women in all fields of development will not only bring justice but humanize the whole development process and make it correspond more to real human needs. This conclusion appears many times in the World Survey and other documents.

... and the challenges for the future

As part of a constructive assessment of contemporary UN thinking concerning women's perspective and participation it might be useful to point out some aspects which seem to be missing or to have received all too little attention so far.

The major shortcoming in all papers on review and assessment of development — whether from women's point of view or otherwise — is the lack of profound and comprehensive criticism and analysis of the philosophy of development and of the concept of development as such. What do we really mean by development? Do we mean merely material and economic development, or do we mean the development of human beings and creation of the best possible social, cultural and material conditions to enable them to unfold their best human qualities and potential?

After a critical analysis of prevailing development philosophy on these grounds we might come to feel a burning need to revise the whole philosophy and concept of development. Then, rather than being ignored, women's culture could appear an untapped, fresh source of skills, values and visions for an alternative path to the future.

There seem to be a few issues which remain constantly untackled or inadequately analysed and elaborated in prevailing discussions and planning. Such issues in the documents of the UNDW are:

— recognition of women's unpaid labour and its importance for the whole of society and for people's well-being;

— the need to change the role of men at the same time as that of women, and thus the distribution of labour between men and women in society and the family;

— issues concerning all aspects of the relationship between human beings and nature.

These issues are substantially interrelated and of great importance to women. They constitute a complex which contemporary Western economic and development thinking seems to have great difficulty with. Is it not a manifestation of the inadequacy of existing economics that it cannot cope with such basic elements in the economy as nature and the different contributions of women?

In this connection the outcome of a recent survey by the UN Non-Governmental Liaison Service, on the interest and concerns of women worldwide regarding the economic crisis and the development of support for alternative approaches and analyses, is very interesting. Structural adjustment and the debt crisis were — not surprisingly — voiced as the overwhelming concern, but second in importance was a call for a quite different, alternative theory and analysis, and reinterpretation of economic, social and political theories and approaches. The need to mobilize women for empowerment and economic independence was also strongly voiced.

The call for the proper recognition of the unpaid labour of women and the whole, non-monetarized economy of households, has been voiced innumerable times during this century. It is called for also in the 1984 World Survey and in the Forward-Looking Strategies, but it is unlikely to be realized unless and until another economics can be created. As John Kenneth Galbraith says in his book *Economics and the Public Purpose:* "The household, in the established economics, is essentially a disguise for the exercise of male authority."[1]

It is often said that, in Western dualistic thinking, women and nature are located in the same category and excluded from the male hemisphere. Nevertheless, the international community seems to have difficulty in seeing the connection between women and nature, and the essential importance of environmental issues to women. The relationships between women and nature are discussed in the FLS in only a few paragraphs in various sub-chapters, and the World Survey and the System-wide Plan also fail to see this connection.

Even the latest authoritative report on the environment and development, *Our Common Future,* does not touch upon the essential connections between women and nature and the immeasurable consequences for women of the deterioration of the environment.[2] The report puts a paramount thrust on the concept of 'sustainable development', but does not sufficiently elaborate on the importance of women in creating it and the potential for women's culture to provide practical, philosophical recipes for the reconstruction of sustainable development.

The connections between women, environment and development could still be made in implementing the System-wide Plan for Women and Development. The creation of a new, alternative economics is the challenge of the century, both to the international community as a whole and to the United Nations System in particular. It is nevertheless a necessity if the economy of nature, or ecology, and the non-monetarized economics of household and mutual neighbourhood co-operation, are to be incorporated into the overall picture of economics. The *Three-Layer Cake with Icing,* by Hazel

Henderson (Figure 4) gives an idea with regard to the way in which the different layers of the human economy are interrelated. 'Mother Nature' and the non-monetized economy are the basis upon which all other economic activities can take place.

Development strategies: the FLS as a new IDS for the 1990's

It seems appropriate to look also at International Development Strategies, past, present and forthcoming, to see to what extent the UN System has incorporated women's interests and contributions into these global strategies for development. The fourth International Development Decade (for the 1990's) will cover the same period as the Nairobi Forward-looking Strategies — the years to 2000.

The goals and objectives of the first UN Development Decade — the 1960's — were so general that it would have been unrealistic to expect any special treatment for women. And those who drafted the International Development Strategy for the Second Development Decade, at the end of the 1960's, still did not realise the importance of women and their role in the development of their countries. Although the Strategy does set somewhat more detailed objectives, coupled with social and cultural goals, it does not mention the contribution of women. The final point in the list of objectives, however, reads: "The full integration of women in the total development effort should be encouraged." That was all in 1970.

At the beginning of the 1970's, with this single sentence as the point of departure, the UN Commission on the Status of Women drew up a more ambitious programme, based on what 'the integration of women in development' should imply in practice. And — despite the shortcomings of the IDS — it was during the Second Development Decade that a great deal of progress on women's issues took place.

Figure 4: Total Productive System of an Industrial Society
(Three-Layer Cake with Icing)

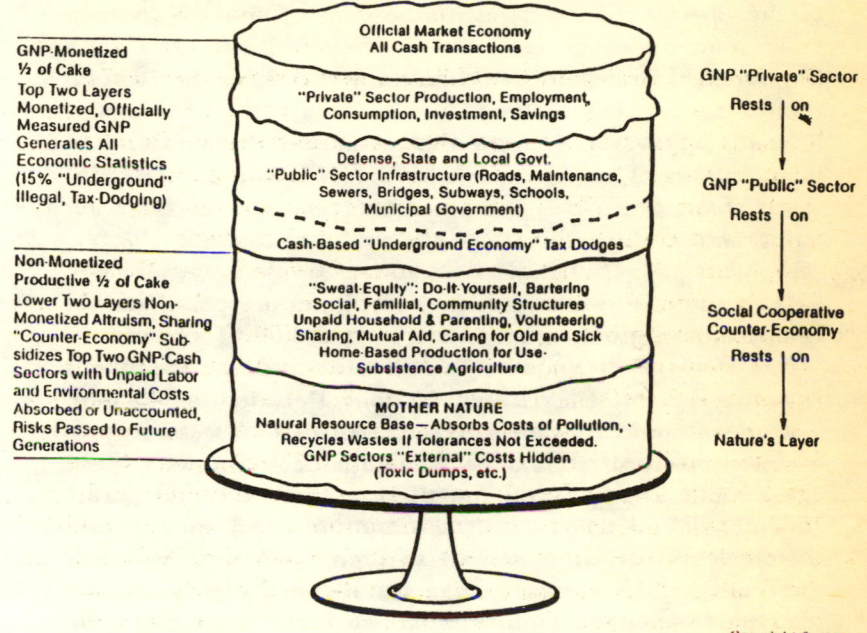

GNP-Monetized ½ of Cake
Top Two Layers Monetized, Officially Measured GNP Generates All Economic Statistics (15% "Underground" Illegal, Tax-Dodging)

Non-Monetized Productive ½ of Cake
Lower Two Layers Non-Monetized Altruism, Sharing "Counter-Economy" Subsidizes Top Two GNP-Cash Sectors with Unpaid Labor and Environmental Costs Absorbed or Unaccounted, Risks Passed to Future Generations

Official Market Economy
All Cash Transactions

"Private" Sector Production, Employment, Consumption, Investment, Savings

Defense, State and Local Govt. **"Public" Sector Infrastructure** (Roads, Maintenance, Sewers, Bridges, Subways, Schools, Municipal Government)

Cash-Based "Underground Economy" Tax Dodges

"Sweat-Equity": Do-It-Yourself, Bartering Social, Familial, Community Structures Unpaid Household & Parenting, Volunteering Sharing, Mutual Aid, Caring for Old and Sick Home-Based Production for Use-Subsistence Agriculture

MOTHER NATURE
Natural Resource Base—Absorbs Costs of Pollution, Recycles Wastes If Tolerances Not Exceeded. GNP Sectors "External" Costs Hidden (Toxic Dumps, etc.)

GNP **"Private" Sector**
Rests | on

GNP **"Public" Sector**
Rests | on

Social Cooperative Counter-Economy
Rests | on

Nature's Layer

The International Development Strategy for the UN's Third Development Decade — the 1980's — is principally based upon the goals of the various Plans of Action adopted by the World Conferences of the 1970's and the long-term objectives of the programmes adopted for future decades by most of the Specialized Agencies and organs of the UN System. Since women's issues had been recognized in many of these programmes during the Women's Decade, there are several points concerning women in the Strategy. Already the Preamble expresses the hope that "a substantial improvement in the status of women will take place during the Decade" and a chapter on Goals and Objectives contains the following paragraph:

"Full and effective participation by the entire population at all stages of the development process should be ensured. In line with the Programme of Action adopted by the World Conference of the United Nations Decade for Women, women should play an active role in that process. Appropriate measures should be taken for profound social and economic changes and for the elimination of the structural imbalances which compound and perpetuate women's disadvantages. To this end, all countries will pursue the objective of *securing women's equal participation both as agents and as beneficiaries in all sectors and at all levels of the development process.* This should include women's greater access to nutrition, health services, education and training, employment, and financial resources and their *greater participation in the analysis, planning, decision-making, implementation and evaluation of development.* Changes that will lead to the *sharing of responsibilities by men and women in the family and in the management of the household should be encouraged.* Institutional and administrative mechanisms to accomplish these objectives should be strengthened. All countries should give high priority to the objectives of mobilizing and integrating youth in development." (Emphasis added by the authors of this book.)

Much still remains unaddressed by this Development Strategy. For example, the chapter on Food and Agriculture lays far less emphasis on the importance and contribution of women than do the final documents from the World Food Conference and the World Conference on Agrarian Reform and Rural Development (which form the basis for this part of the Strategy), thus manifesting the traditionally haphazard recognition accorded to women.

The Mexico and Copenhagen Plans of Action are referred to only briefly, in a small paragraph at the end of the chapter on Social Development. Unlike the other Plans of Action, their substance is not incorporated in the Strategy; it is merely mentioned that "the important set of measures to improve the status of women (contained in the above-mentioned Plans of Action) should be implemented".

If the points of substance concerning women in the IDS for the 1980's were just a fraction of what they were in the plans and programmes on which the IDS was based, they are even more so in the mid-term review and appraisal made in 1985.[3] Women are mentioned only in connection with social objectives and social development, indicating that still, in the middle of the 1980's, the authors of this report considered women merely as 'social cases' needing care and services, not as participants and contributors to the economy. Only in connection with farming is there a glimpse of another approach; "Ensuring that small and women farmers have access to credit and inputs, and providing security of tenure, could be as important as developing new seed varieties."

Only at the end of the document are there direct references to the Nairobi Conference and review and appraisal of the UN Decade for Women. It is recognized that even "previously hard-won gains in women's access to employment, to better working conditions and to the benefits of various social programmes" have been threatened with reversal due to the economic crisis. There would have been plenty of material on women for the appraisal of the Third Development Decade if they had used the review and appraisal undertaken for the Nairobi Conference.

But surprisingly enough there is one problem expressed very clearly, both in the IDS and in its review and appraisal, which is missing in the Forward-looking Strategies and the System-wide Plan: the more equitable sharing by men and women "in the management of the household", not only "parental and family responsibilities". Management of the household undoubtedly includes also the carrying of water and collection of fuel!

In the review and appraisal of the IDS it is made very clear:

> "Women in developing countries remain a disadvantaged group, often carrying a disproportionate share of the burden of home and family responsibilities. This burden is particularly heavy for women in rural areas, where there is no clear distinction between economic and domestic activities. Added to this is a traditional, strong patriarchal value system that favours sexually segregated roles in the household and the family, giving only a marginal role to women in family decision-making and property ownership" (paragraph 154).

Preparations for the IDS for the Fourth Development Decade (1990's) are already in progress within the respective bodies of the United Nations. What will be the role of the Forward-looking Strategies and the System-wide Medium-term Plan for Women and Development in this process? Common/woman-sense would say that they would provide timely, well-prepared basic documents for this IDS. The FLS as such already constitute a development strategy for the decade 1990-2000. The System-wide Plan shows how to implement those strategies within the whole UN system in the first part of the decade.

The first paper on the preparation of a new development strategy was prepared for the 43rd Session of the General Assembly (A/43/376). The Forward-looking Strategies for the Advancement of Women were not even mentioned in the document, in spite of the fact that they were unanimously adopted by the same governments preparing the IDS. Neither are preparations for the IDS mentioned in the System-wide Medium-term Plan (1990-1995). The question arises: how can we coordinate — how can we persuade governments to coordinate — these processes so that a lot of unnecessary work can be avoided and a better IDS for the 1990's be produced?

Positive examples

There are, however, many positive examples in the UN System of serious efforts to implement and take further the decisions of Nairobi. Concrete examples are, for example, the Inter-Organizational Top Management Seminar on Women and Development held in 1986, a comprehensive UNDP Programme Advisory Note, and the Food Aid Strategies for Women and Development of the World Food Programme.

The *Top Management Seminar* was organized in December 1986 by the Joint Consultative Group on Policy (JCGP) of UNDP, UNICEF, the UN Population Fund and the World Food Programme. Organization of such a seminar, and personal participation of top-level managers of these organizations, was a clear indication of their commitment to do something in practice and also of their awareness of the need to study the issue of women and development more thoroughly. The aim of the seminar was "to ensure that women are incorporated into these organizations' mainstream development activities".

The report of the seminar[4] speaks very clearly about what, in the past work of these organizations concerning women, has been omitted, what has failed, and why. It also reveals familiar misunderstandings and misinterpretations of women and development issues. It then gives policy directives for the rectification of these shortcomings, advice on methods, and establishes a priority order for practical action. It also includes a list of actions to be taken jointly by the JCGP organizations. At the end of the report the Executive Heads of the organizations express their commitments in quite a concrete manner.

These organizations have all proved their seriousness with regard to the advancement of women; all have a history of such efforts over several years, both before and after the Top Management Seminar. One of the indications of this seriousness is the thoroughly prepared, comprehensive *Programme Advisory Note on Women in Development*, issued by UNDP and adopted in 1986.[5] It was prepared in collaboration with all agencies executing UNDP-funded projects in the field (FAO, IFAD, ILO, UNCDF, UN/DTCD, Unesco, UNFPA, UNICEF, UNIDO, UNIFEM, the World Bank, WFP and WHO — see

list of acronyms and addresses). It is directed to governments, to the UN development system and to non-governmental organisations involved in supporting efforts to
accelerate economic and social development for the benefit of
the entire populations of their countries.

The Note is intended to assist development officials of all
kinds to deal with issues related to women's role in, and
contribution to, development and to enhance the quality and
effectiveness of development assistance for the benefit of
women.

The profound commitment to women and development of
an organization such as the World Food Programme may
not be too well known, and may even be unexpected. But a
document prepared for the WFP Committee on Food Aid
Policies and Programmes on food aid strategies for women
in development (WFP/CFA:23/7) in 1987 is a convincing
indication of thorough work done on this issue in this organization, and perhaps also of the inspiration and stimulus
of the Top Management Seminar.

The document is worthy of mention here for its clear picture of reality and its insights into ways of improving the situation of women:

> "Women are involved in development everywhere and all
> the time. The point is to create conditions under which
> women can be involved in social and economic transfor-
> mation on better terms ... the involvement of women in
> the development process is not just a matter of ethics but of
> good economics."

The document speaks of "the strategic role of women in the
economy", which was recognized in WFP already in 1975:

> "A focus on gender does not proceed from a concern with
> inequalities between men and women, but on the recogni-
> tion of differences between men and women in relation to
> household division of labour, access to and control over
> production resources and assets, and stakes and in-
> centives."

The Committee on Food Aid Policies and Programmes fully
endorsed the policy principles in the document, and requested the secretariat to prepare a plan of action to promote
the application of the policy.

These examples give just a hint about what is going on in practice in the fields of the various UN organizations. We have to recognize, however, that introducing such thorough-going new principles and practical guidelines as these is a time-consuming and strenuous process. One has to be prepared to work for years by means of staff training, expert education, data collection, programme monitoring and evaluation, etc., before the results are likely to be an overall feature of the development process.

In any event, the guidelines and programme papers are necessary first tools to get the process started. They are also very informative and useful learning materials for those studying women and development issues and the efforts made within the UN System.

How to make it happen?

We have now learned a lot about measures and programmes within the UN System intended to ensure that the provisions and recommendations of the Nairobi FLS will be implemented. But the UN is just an instrument of governments; international multilateral co-operation is a continuous process, in which very few things take place automatically. We need procedures, mechanisms and policies to keep the process going, and monitoring to ensure that it is going in the right direction.

National governments

The main actors in the arena of multilateral, intergovernmental co-operation are national governments. They have an obligation to act, both at international level and at their respective national, domestic levels. They are the agents for putting UN decisions into effect. If governments do not implement the decisions they have agreed upon in the UN, nothing happens. The UN System has neither the means nor the mandate to make things happen without the support of member states.

So all the provisions of the Nairobi FLS, as well as the programmes and recommendations adopted thereafter, are as mandatory upon national governments as upon the United Nations. Governments have to make them part of their policies in legislation, in economic and social policies, in culture, education and training as well as in public discussion and communication in their countries.

We have seen, in earlier chapters, how far the UN has already come in its commitment to implement the Nairobi FLS and the Convention on the Elimination of All Forms of Discrimination against Women. At the moment the problem is, indeed, at the governmental level. The first review and appraisal of the implementation of the NFLS in member countries was due to take place at the beginning of 1989. Member governments were requested to report on their actions and measures to implement the Strategies. By the time the deadline was reached, only about 30 countries had returned the questionnaires and, of them, fewer than 20 contained any substantial information. This seems to indicate either that the member states have not done much to implement the decisions they adopted in Nairobi, or that they cannot be bothered to reply to UN enquiries.

It would seem that there is a lot to be done in each country to create the concerned and firm political will required to implement the unanimous decisions made within the UN System. And a coordinated and appropriate system and policy is also needed to ensure that each country acts consistently on issues of concern to women at the international level, in all the various organs and agencies of the UN System. (See box; also Annex 3: Organizations that have agreed to implement the System-wide Medium-term Plan for Women and Development.)

The ultimate power lies with the people

The means at the disposal of the UN System to press sovereign governments to implement their joint decisions are very limited. The final responsibility lies with the people of each country.

> "... the ultimate strength of the Organization and its capacity to promote and achieve the objectives for which it has been established lie in the degree to which its aims

and activities are understood and supported by the peoples of the world".

The words of then-Secretary-General U Thant in 1966 are still valid, and concern also the issues discussed in this book. In fact, they imply the principle of the peoples' responsibility to see to it that governments implement the resolutions and recommendations they have adopted within the UN System.

The key actors in this case are, in particular, women and their organizations in each country. They have to study in depth the provisions of the FLS and the Convention, because these documents give leverage to their insistence that governments keep the promises given when adopting these documents. It is dialectics of this kind between people and their governments which make international machinery work.

Major steps to be taken by women's organizations, together with national institutions for the advancement of women, are the following:

— to see to it that the Nairobi Forward-Looking Strategies and the Convention on the Elimination of All Forms of Discrimination against Women are translated into national languages (in countries not speaking any of the official languages of the UN), and are widely distributed and studied by the citizens and relevant officials of the country;

— together with other NGOs, political parties and the women's movement, to press their respective governments to implement these documents, since they concern more than half of the citizens in each country and form a comprehensive programme for peace, equality and more humane and sustainable development.

— to do everything possible to ensure that their respective governments also support the comprehensive efforts of the UN System to implement the Nairobi FLS at the international level.

But women need not restrict themselves to promoting and following-up what is stipulated in the documents and resolutions adopted in the past. The women's movement is a living process, carried forward and supported by ever-expanding feminist research. At the moment feminism is about to shape itself into a social and political philosophy of its own, encompassing three basic elements: equality, ecology and peace. Development, as one of the basic elements of the NFLS, is the process towards these aims. This gives the women's movement the potential to expand and refine social and political thinking, and to bring a constant flow of new substance and depth into the development process.

This progress in the thinking and philosophy of the world's women should, and will be, reflected also in the intergovernmental process and the United Nations System. The dialectical process will go on. It will develop further the principles and measures to bring forward the aims of the NFLS and the Convention on the Elimination of All Forms of Discrimination against Women, i.e. the advancement of women and their equal participation in political decision-making and all forms of progress. And it will bring new issues onto the agenda, and new connotations to the decisions of the UN System, in the course of time.

This book can serve, hopefully, as a stepping stone in this process of finding out how the United Nations System can continue to provide leverage and assistance to women around the world in claiming their rights and assuming their share of power. Women's equitable participation in all walks of life, nationally and internationally, is no longer only their legitimate right but a social and political necessity in the process towards a more balanced, humane and sustainable future. We live in a time when women really do matter in world development.

Notes

[1] John Kenneth Galbraith, *Economics and the Public Purpose.* Houghton Mifflin, Boston, 1973.

[2] *Our Common Future.* World Commission on Environment and Development Oxford University Press, 1987.

[3] *Review and Appraisal of the Implementation of the International Development Strategy for the Third United Nations Development Decade.* A/AC.219/36.29, August 1985.

[4] *Report of the Inter-Organizational Top Management Seminar on Women and Development,* New York, 18-19 December 1986. UN Joint Consultative Group on Policy (UNDP, UNICEF, UNFPA (UNPF) and WFP.

[5] *Women in Development.* UNDP Programme Advisory Note, *op.cit.*

A Proposal for the Coordination of International Women's Programmes in National Foreign Policy

If a government wishes to behave consistently in its policies on a specific subject matter, it has to present and promote the same logic in a corresponding manner in all of the Specialized Agencies and bodies of the UN System. In order to promote the advancement of women and implementation of the Nairobi Forward-looking Strategies systematically at international fora, it needs to have a coherent policy, to train and brief its diplomats and representatives in all international bodies accordingly, and to have a coordinating system within the domestic administration to manage and facilitate the systematic policies and representation of the country concerning these issues.

Such coordination and systematic conduct of policies could be organized in different ways in different national administrations. The following is one possible model: to develop an integrated, system-wide approach, and manifest the country's firm commitment to the advancement of women and the elimination of gender-based discrimination, *an International Equality Unit or a Principal Officer* could be established within the national administration (in the Ministry of Foreign Affairs, Office of the Prime Minister, or other appropriate structure) with the mandate to:

a)   draw up strategic guidelines for the implementation of international measures outlined in the FLS;

b)   follow up the implementation of the FLS in the international system and instruct the decision-makers and representatives of the country accordingly;

c)   ensure the substantive input of the country to advancement of women issues at key international meetings and conferences;

d)   coordinate and guide the responsible departmental officials in respective ministries and national boards, as well as the permanent missions of the country to the UN agencies and organs.

e)   propose appropriate and necessary allocations of funds for the United Nations institutions and organs for advancement of women, and for the necessary functions to promote these issues in the domestic administration;

f)   establish and chair a national ad hoc interdepartmental steering committee to facilitate the accomplishment of these aims.

The Unit or Officer should be assisted by corresponding contact officials/focal points/links in different departments, ministries and national boards. This is particularly important in the case of the Ministry or Agency for Development Cooperation/Planning, to guide and monitor programmes and policies on women and development. This kind of co-ordinating system at the country level corresponds to the UN Administrative Committee on Coordination and would facilitate its role in the implementation of the NFLS within the UN System. The System-wide Medium-term Plans for Women and Development 1990-1995 and 1996-2001 provide a comprehensive frame of reference also for the national co-ordination of policies on international issues of concern to women.

List of Acronyms and Addresses

(Contact person for Women's Questions in parentheses)

CSDHA
: UN Centre for Social Development and Humanitarian Affairs, Vienna International Centre, PO Box 500, A-1400 Vienna. Tel: 21131. (Ms. C. Sellami-Meslem).

CSTD
: UN Centre for Science and Technology for Development, (DCI 1022) United Nations, New York, NY 10017. Tel: (212) 963.1234. (Ms. Hiroko Morita-Lou).

DAW
: Division for the Advancement of Women, CSDHA (see above).

DIESA
: UN Dept. of International Economic and Social Affairs, United Nations, New York, NY 10017. Tel: (212) 963.1234. (Ms. Joann Vanek, Statistics).

DPI
: UN Dept. of Public Information, United Nations, New York, NY 10017. Tel: (212) 963.1234 (Ms. Susan Markham)

ECA
: Economic Commission for Africa, PO Box 3001, Addis Abeba, Ethiopia. Tel: 44.72.00-44.70.00. (Ms. Mary Tadesse).

ECLAC
: Economic Commission for Latin-America and the Caribbean, Edificio Naciones Unidas, Avenida Dag Hammarskjöld, Bitacura, Santiago, Chile. Tel: 485051-485061. (Ms. Miriam Krawczyk).

FAO
: Food and Agriculture Organization of the United Nations, Via Terme di Caracalla, 00100 Rome. Tel: 57951 (Dr. Anita Spring).

IAEA
: International Atomic Energy Agency, Vienna International Centre, PO Box 100, A-1400 Vienna. (Ms. Frances Mautner-Markhof)

IBRD
: World Bank (International Bank for Reconstruction and Development), 1818 H. Street, N.W., Washington DC 20433. Tel: (202) 477.1234. (Ms. Barbara K. Herz).

IFAD
: International Fund for Agricultural Development, Via del Serafico 107, 00142 Rome. Tel: 54591. (Ms. Natalie Hahn).

ILO
: International Labour Organization, 4, route des Morillons, 1211 Geneva 22. Tel: 799.61.11. (Ms. S.C. Cornwell).

INCB
: International Narcotics Control Board, Vienna International Centre, PO Box 500, A-1400 Vienna. Tel: 21131. (Ms. Marie T.Kuesell).

INSTRAW
: International Research and Training Institute for the Advancement of Women, Apartado Postal 21747, Santo Domingo, Dominican Republic. Tel: 685.2111. (Ms.Dunja Pastizzi-Ferencic).

NGLS	UN Non-Governmental Liaison Service, Palais des Nations, 1211 Geneva 10. Tel: 734.60.11. (Ms. Yvonne Backholm).
UNCHR	UN Centre for Human Rights, Palais des Nations, 1211 Geneva 10. Tel: 734.60.11. (Ms. Yolande Diallo).
UNCTAD	UN Conference on Trade and Development, Palais des Nations, 1211 Geneva 10. Tel: 734.60.11. (Mr. I. Erchov).
UNDP	UN Development Programme, One United Nations Plaza, New York, NY 10017. Tel: (212) 906.5000. (Ms. Elizabeth Reid).
UNDRC	UN Disaster Relief Coordinator, Palais des Nations, 1211 Geneva 10, Tel: (4122) 731.02.11. (Ms. Odette Mengin)
UNEP	UN Environment Programme, PO Box 30552, Nairobi, Kenya. Tel: 333930. (Ms. Monique Mainguet).
Unesco	United Nations Educational, Scientific and Cultural Organization, 7, Place de Fontenoy, 75700 Paris. Tel: (1) 4568.10.00. (Ms. Merete Gerlach-Nielsen).
UNFPA	United Nations Population Fund, 220 East 42nd St., New York, NY 10017. Tel: (212) 850.5792. (Ms. Mehri Hekmati).
UNHCR	UN High Commissioner for Refugees, Case Postal, CH 1211 Geneva 2 Dépot. Tel: 739.8111. (Ms. Ann Brazeau).
UNICEF	UN Children's Fund, 3, United Nations Plaza, New York, NY 10017. Tel: (212) 326.7000. (Ms. Agnes Aidoo).
UNIDO	United Nations Industrial Development Organization, PO Box 300, A-1400 Vienna. Tel: 21131. (Ms. B. Chambalu)
UNIDR	United Nations Institute for Disarmament Research, Room A-210, Palais des Nations, 1211 Geneva 10. Tel: 734.60.11. (Ms. C. de Jonge Oudraat).
UNIFEM	United Nations Development Fund for Women, c/o UNDP. (Ms. Sharon Capeling-Alakija).
UNITAR	UN Institute for Training and Research, 801 United Nations Plaza, New York, NY 10017. Tel: (212) 754.8622-8637.
UNRISD	UN Research Institute for Social Development, Palais des Nations,1211 Geneva 10. Tel: 798.84.00. (Ms.C.Hewitt de Alcantara).
UNRWA	UN Relief and Works Agency for Palestine Refugees in the Near East, Vienna International Centre, PO Box 700, A-1400 Vienna. Tel: 21131. (Mr. Jesper Knudsen).
WFC	World Food Council, Via Terme di Caracalla, 00100 Rome. Tel: 57971. (Mr. Alain Vidal-Naquet).
WFP	World Food Programme, Via Terme di Caracalla, 00100 Rome. Tel: 57971. (Ms. Mona Hammam).
WHO	World Health Organization, 20 Avenue Appia, 1211 Geneva 27. Tel: 792.21.11 (Dr. Brigitte Gredler).

Annexes

Annex 1

Convention on the Elimination of All Forms of Discrimination against Women

Adopted and opened for signature, ratification and accession by General Assembly resolution 34/180 of 18 December 1979

ENTRY INTO FORCE: 3 September 1981, in accordance with article 27 (i).

The States Parties to the present Convention,

Noting that the Charter of the United Nations reaffirms faith in fundamental human rights, in the dignity and worth of the human person and in the equal rights of men and women,

Noting that the Universal Declaration of Human Rights affirms the principle of the inadmissibility of discrimination and proclaims that all human beings are born free and equal in dignity and rights and that everyone is entitled to all the rights and freedoms set forth therein, without distinction of any kind, including distinction based on sex,

Noting that the States Parties to the International Covenants on Human Rights have the obligation to ensure the equal right of men and women to enjoy all economic, social, cultural, civil and political rights,

Considering the international conventions concluded under the auspices of the United Nations and the specialized agencies promoting equality of rights of men and women,

Noting also the resolutions, declarations and recommendations adopted by the United Nations and the specialized agencies promoting equality of rights of men and women,

Concerned, however, that despite these various instruments extensive discrimination against women continues to exist,

Recalling that discrimination against women violates the principles of equality of rights and respect for human dignity, is an obstacle to the participation of women, on equal terms with men, in the political, social, economic and cultural life of their countries, hampers the growth of the prosperity of society and the family and makes more difficult the full development of the potentialities of women in the service of their countries and of humanity,

Concerned that in situations of poverty women have the least access to food, health, education, training and opportunities for employment and other needs,

Convinced that the establishment of the new international economic order based on equity and justice will contribute significantly towards the promotion of equality between men and women,

Emphasizing that the eradication of *apartheid*, all forms of racism, racial discrimination, colonialism, neo-colonialism, aggression, foreign occupation and domination and interference in the internal affairs of States is essential to the full enjoyment of the rights of men and women,

Affirming that the strengthening of international peace and security, the relaxation of international tension, mutual co-operation among all States irrespective of their social and economic systems, general and complete disarmament, in particular nuclear disarmament under strict and effective international control, the affirmation of the principles of justice, equality and mutual benefit in relations among countries and the realization of the right of peoples under alien and colonial domination and foreign occupation to self-determination and independence, as well as respect for national sovereignty and territorial integrity, will promote social progress and development and as a consequence will contribute to the attainment of full equality between men and women,

Convinced that the full and complete development of a country, the welfare of the world and the cause of peace require the maximum participation of women on equal terms with men in all fields,

Bearing in mind the great contribution of women to the welfare of the family and to the development of society, so far not fully recognized, the social significance of maternity and the role of both parents in the family and in the upbringing of children, and aware that the role of women in procreation should not be a basis for discrimination but that the upbringing of children requires a sharing of responsibility between men and women and society as a whole,

Aware that a change in the traditional role of men as well as the role of women in society and in the family is needed to achieve full equality between men and women,

Determined to implement the principles set forth in the Declaration on the Elimination of Discrimination against Women and, for that purpose, to adopt the measures required for the elimination of such discrimination in all its forms and manifestions,

Have agreed on the following:

Part I

Article 1

For the purposes of the present Convention, the term "discrimination against women" shall mean any distinction, exclusion or restriction made on the basis of sex which has the effect or purpose of impairing or nullifying the recognition, enjoyment or exercise by women, irrespective of their marital status, on a basis of equality of men and women, of human rights and fundamental freedoms in the political, economic, social, cultural, civil or any other field.

Article 2

States Parties condemn discrimination against women in all its forms, agree to pursue by all appropriate means and without delay a policy of eliminating discrimination against women and, to this end, undertake:

(*a*) To embody the principle of the equality of men and women in their national constitutions or other appropriate legislation if not yet incorporated therein and to ensure, through law and other appropriate means, the practical realization of this principle;

(*b*) To adopt appropriate legislative and other measures, incuding sanctions where appropriate, prohibiting all discrimination against women;

(*c*) To establish legal protection of the rights of women on an equal basis with men and to ensure through competent national tribunals and other public institutions the effective protection of women against any act of discrimination;

(*d*) To refrain from engaging in any act or practice of discrimination against women and to ensure that public authorities and institutions shall act in conformity with this obligation;

(*e*) To take all appropriate measures to eliminate discrimination against women by any person, organization or enterprise;

(*f*) To take all appropriate measures, including legislation, to modify or abolish existing laws, regulations, customs and practices which constitute discrimination against women;

(*g*) To repeal all national penal provisions which constitute discrimination against women.

Article 3

State Parties shall take in all fields, in particular in the political, social, economic and cultural fields, all appropriate measures, including legislation, to ensure the full development and advancement of women, for the purpose of guaranteeing them the exercise and enjoyment of human rights and fundamental freedoms on a basis of equality with men.

Article 4

1. Adoption by States Parties of temporary special measures aimed at accelerating *de facto* equality between men and women shall not be considered discrimination as defined in the present Convention, but shall in no way entail as a consequence the maintenance of unequal or separate standards; these measures shall be discontinued when the objectives of equality of opportunity and treatment have been achieved.

2. Adoption by States Parties of special measures, including those measures contained in the present Convention, aimed at protecting maternity shall not be considered discriminatory.

Article 5

States Parties shall take all appropriate measures:

(*a*) To modify the social and cultural patterns of conduct of men and women, with a view to achieving the elimination of prejudices and customary and all other practices which are based on the idea of the inferiority or the superiority of either of the sexes or on stereotyped roles for men and women;

(*b*) To ensure that family education includes a proper understanding of maternity as a social function and the recognition of the common responsibility of men and women in the upbringing and development of their children, it being understood that the interest of the children is the primordial consideration in all cases.

Article 6

States Parties shall take all appropriate measures, including legislation, to suppress all forms of traffic in women and exploitation of prostitution of women.

Part II

Article 7

States Parties shall take all appropriate measures to eliminate discrimination against women in the political and public life of the country and, in particular, shall ensure to women, on equal terms with men, the right:

(*a*) To vote in all elections and public referenda and to be eligible for election to all publicly elected bodies;

(*b*) To participate in the formulation of government policy and the implementation thereof and to hold public office and perform all public functions at all levels of government;

(*c*) To participate in non-governmental organizations and associations concerned with the public and political life of the country.

Article 8

States Parties shall take all appropriate measures to ensure to women, on equal terms with men and without any discrimination, the opportunity to represent their Governments at the international level and to participate in the work of international organizations.

Article 9

1. States Parties shall grant women equal rights with men to acquire, change or retain their nationality. They shall ensure in particular that neither marriage to an alien nor change of nationality by the husband during marriage shall automatically change the nationality of the wife, render her stateless or force upon her the nationality of the husband.

2. States Parties shall grant women equal rights with men with respect to the nationality of their children.

Part III

Article 10

States Parties shall take all appropriate measures to eliminate discrimination against women in order to ensure to them equal rights with men in the field of education and in particular to ensure, on a basis of equality of men and women:

(*a*) The same conditions for career and vocational guidance, for access to studies and for the achievement of diplomas in educational establishments of all categories in rural as well as in urban areas; this equality shall be ensured in pre-school, general, technical, professional and higher technical education, as well as in all types of vocational training;

(*b*) Access to the same curricula, the same examinations, teaching staff with qualifications of the same standard and school premises and equipment of the same quality;

(*c*) The elimination of any stereotyped concept of the roles of men and women at all levels and in all forms of education by encouraging coeducation and other types of education which will help to achieve this aim and, in particular, by the revision of textbooks and school programmes and the adaptation of teaching methods;

(*d*) The same opportunities to benefit from scholarships and other study grants;

(*e*) The same opportunities for access to programmes of continuing education, including adult and functional literacy programmes, particularly those aimed at reducing, at the earliest possible time, any gap in education existing between men and women;

(*f*) The reduction of female student drop-out rates and the organization of programmes for girls and women who have left school prematurely;

(*g*) The same opportunities to participate actively in sports and physical education;

(*h*) Access to specific educational information to help to ensure the health and well-being of families, including information and advice on family planning.

Article 11

1. States Parties shall take all appropriate measures to eliminate discrimination against women in the field of employment in order to ensure, on a basis of equality of men and women, the same rights, in particular:

(*a*) The right to work as an inalienable right of all human beings;

(*b*) The right to the same employment opportunities, including the application of the same criteria for selection in matters of employment;

(*c*) The right to free choice of profession and employment, the right to promotion, job security and all benefits and conditions of service and the right to receive vocational training and retraining, including apprenticeships, advanced vocational training and recurrent training;

(*d*) The right to equal remuneration, including benefits, and to equal treatment in respect of work of equal value, as well as equality of treatment in the evaluation of the quality of work;

(*e*) The right to social security, particularly in cases of retirement, unemployment, sickness, invalidity and old age and other incapacity to work, as well as the right to paid leave;

(*f*) The right to protection of health and to safety in working conditions, including the safeguarding of the function of reproduction.

2. In order to prevent discrimination against women on the grounds of marriage or maternity and to ensure their effective right to work, States Parties shall take appropriate measures:

(*a*) To prohibit, subject to the imposition of sanctions, dismissal on the grounds of pregnancy or of maternity leave and discrimination in dismissals on the basis of marital status;

(*b*) To introduce maternity leave with pay or with comparable social benefits without loss of former employment, seniority or social allowances;

(*c*) To encourage the provision of the necessary supporting social services to enable parents to combine family obligations with work responsibilities and participation in public life, in particular through promoting the establishment and development of a network of child-care facilities;

(*d*) To provide special protection to women during pregnancy in types of work proved to be harmful to them.

3. Protective legislation relating to matters covered in this article shall be reviewed periodically in the light of scientific and technological knowledge and shall be revised, repealed or extended as necessary.

Article 12

1. States Parties shall take all appropriate measures to eliminate discrimination against women in the field of health care in order to ensure, on a basis of equality of men and women, access to health care services, including those related to family planning.

2. Notwithstanding the provisions of paragraph 1 of this article, States Parties shall ensure to women appropriate services in connexion with pregnancy, confinement and the post-natal period, granting free services where necessary, as well as adequate nutrition during pregnancy and lactation.

Article 13

States Parties shall take all appropriate measures to eliminate discrimination against women in other areas of economic and social life in order to ensure, on a basis of equality of men and women, the same rights, in particular:

(*a*) The right to family benefits;

(*b*) The right to bank loans, mortgages and other forms of financial credit;

(*c*) The right to participate in recreational activities, sports and all aspects of cultural life.

Article 14

1. States Parties shall take into account the particular problems faced by rural women and the significant roles which rural women play in the economic survival of their families, including their work in the non-monetized sectors of the economy, and shall take all appropriate measures to ensure the application of the provisions of the present Convention to women in rural areas.

2. States Parties shall take all appropriate measures to eliminate discrimination against women in rural areas in order to ensure, on a basis of equality of men and women, that they participate in and benefit from rural development and, in particular, shall ensure to such women the right:

(*a*) To participate in the elaboration and implementation of development planning at all levels;

(*b*) To have access to adequate health care facilities, including information, counselling and services in family planning;

(*c*) To benefit directly from social security programmes;

(*d*) To obtain all types of training and education, formal and non-formal, including that relating to functional literacy, as well as, *inter alia*, the benefit of all community and extension services, in order to increase their technical proficiency;

(*e*) To organize self-help groups and co-operatives in order to obtain equal access to economic opportunities through employment or self-employment;

(*f*) To participate in all community activities;

(*g*) To have access to agricultural credit and loans, marketing facilities, appropriate technology and equal treatment in land and agrarian reform as well as in land resettlement schemes;

(*h*) To enjoy adequate living conditions, particularly in relation to housing, sanitation, electricity and water supply, transport and communications.

Part IV

Article 15

1. States Parties shall accord to women equality with men before the law.

2. States Parties shall accord to women, in civil matters, a legal capacity identical to that of men and the same opportunities to exercise that capacity. In particular, they shall give women equal rights to conclude contracts and to administer property and shall treat them equally in all stages of procedure in courts and tribunals.

3. States Parties agree that all contracts and all other private instruments of any kind with a legal effect which is directed at restricting the legal capacity of women shall be deemed null and void.

4. States Parties shall accord to men and women the same rights with regard to the law relating to the movement of persons and the freedom to choose their residence and domicile.

Article 16

1. States Parties shall take all appropriate measures to eliminate discrimination against women in all matters relating to marriage and family relations and in particular shall ensure, on a basis of equality of men and women:

(*a*) The same right to enter into marriage;

(*b*) The same right freely to choose a spouse and to enter into marriage only with their free and full consent;

(*c*) The same rights and responsibilities during marriage and at its dissolution;

(*d*) The same rights and responsibilities as parents, irrespective of their marital status, in matters relating to their children; in all cases the interests of the children shall be paramount;

(*e*) The same rights to decide freely and responsibly on the number and spacing of their children and to have access to the information, education and means to enable them to exercise these rights;

(*f*) The same rights and responsibilities with regard to guardianship, wardship, trusteeship and adoption of children, or similar institutions where these concepts exist in national legislation; in all cases the interests of the children shall be paramount;

(*g*) The same personal rights as husband and wife, including the right to choose a family name, a profession and an occupation;

(*h*) The same rights for both spouses in respect of the ownership, acquisition, management, administration, enjoyment and disposition of property, whether free of charge or for a valuable consideration.

2. The betrothal and the marriage of a child shall have no legal effect, and all necessary

action, including legislation, shall be taken to specify a minimum age for marriage and to make the registration of marriages in an official registry compulsory.

Part V

Article 17

1.   For the purpose of considering the progress made in the implementation of the present Convention, there shall be established a Committee on the Elimination of Discrimination against Women (hereinafter referred to as the Committee) consisting, at the time of entry into force of the Convention, of eighteen and, after ratification of or accession to the Convention by the thirty-fifth State Party, of twenty-three experts of high moral standing and competence in the field covered by the Convention. The experts shall be elected by States Parties from among their nationals and shall serve in their personal capacity, consideration being given to equitable geographical distribution and to the representation of the different forms of civilization as well as the principal legal systems.

2.   The members of the Committee shall be elected by secret ballot from a list of persons nominated by States Parties. Each State Party may nominate one person from among its own nationals.

3.   The initial election shall be held six months after the date of the entry into force of the present Convention. At least three months before the date of each election the Secretary-General of the United Nations shall address a letter to the States Parties inviting them to submit their nominations within two months. The Secretary-General shall prepare a list in alphabetical order of all persons thus nominated, indicating the States Parties which have nominated them, and shall submit it to the States Parties.

4.   Elections of the members of the Committee shall be held at a meeting of States Parties convened by the Secretary-General at United Nations Headquarters. At that meeting, for which two thirds of the States Parties shall constitute a quorum, the persons elected to the Committee shall be those nominees who obtain the largest number of votes and an absolute majority of the votes of the representatives of States Parties present and voting.

5.   The members of the Committee shall be elected for a term of four years. However, the terms of nine of the members elected at the first election shall expire at the end of two years; immediately after the first election the names of these nine members shall be chosen by lot by the Chairman of the Committee.

6.   The election of the five additional members of the Committee shall be held in accordance with the provisions of paragraphs 2, 3 and 4 of this article, following the thirty-fifth ratification or accession. The terms of two of the additional members elected on this occasion shall expire at the end of two years, the names of these two members having been chosen by lot by the Chairman of the Committee.

7.   For the filling of casual vacancies, the State Party whose expert has ceased to function as a member of the Committee shall appoint another expert from among its nationals, subject to the approval of the Committee.

8.   The members of the Committee shall, with the approval of the General Assembly, receive emoluments from United Nations resources on such terms and conditions as the Assembly may decide, having regard to the importance of the Committee's responsibilities.

9.   The Secretary-General of the United Nations shall provide the necessary staff and facilities for the effective performance of the functions of the Committee under the present Convention.

Article 18

1.   States Parties undertake to submit to the Secretary-General of the United Nations, for consideration by the Committee, a report on the legislative, judicial, administrative or other measures which they have adopted to give effect to the provisions of the present Convention and on the progress made in this respect:

(*a*) Within one year after the entry into force for the State concerned;

(*b*) Thereafter at least every four years and further whenever the Committee so requests.

2.   Reports may indicate factors and difficulties affecting the degree of fulfilment of obligations under the present Convention.

Article 19

   1. The Committee shall adopt its own rules of procedure.

   2. The Committee shall elect its officers for a term of two years.

Article 20

   1. The Committee shall normally meet for a period of not more than two weeks annually in order to consider the reports submitted in accordance with article 18 of the present Convention.

   2. The meetings of the Committee shall normally be held at United Nations Headquarters or at any other convenient place as determined by the Committee.

Article 21

   1. The Committee shall, through the Economic and Social Council, report annually to the General Assembly of the United Nations on its activities and may make suggestions and general recommendations based on the examination of reports and information received from the States Parties. Such suggestions and general recommendations shall be included in the report of the Committee together with comments, if any, from States Parties.

   2. The Secretary-General of the United Nations shall transmit the reports of the Committee to the Commission on the Status of Women for its information.

Article 22

The specialized agencies shall be entitled to be represented at the consideration of the implementation of such provisions of the present Convention as fall within the scope of their activities. The Committee may invite the specialized agencies to submit reports on the implementation of the Convention in areas falling within the scope of their activities.

Part VI

Article 23

Nothing in the present Convention shall affect any provisions that are more conducive to the achievement of equality between men and women which may be contained:

   (*a*) In the leglisation of a State Party; or

   (*b*) In any other international convention, treaty or agreement in force for that State.

Article 24

State Parties undertake to adopt all necessary measures at the national level aimed at achieving the full realization of the rights recognized in the present Convention.

Article 25

   1. The present Convention shall be open for signature by all States.

   2. The Secretary-General of the United Nations is designated as the depositary of the present Convention.

   3. The present Convention is subject to ratification. Instruments of ratification shall be deposited with the Secretary-General of the United Nations.

   4. The present Convention shall be open to accession by all States. Accession shall be effected by the deposit of an instrument of accession with the Secretary-General of the United Nations.

Article 26

   1. A request for the revision of the present Convention may be made at any time by any State Party by means of a notification in writing addressed to the Secretary-General of the United Nations.

   2. The General Assembly of the United Nations shall decide upon the steps, if any, to be taken in respect of such a request.

Article 27

   1. The present Convention shall enter into force on the thirtieth day after the date of deposit with the Secretary-General of the United Nations of the twentieth instrument of ratification or accession.

   2. For each State ratifying the present Convention or acceding to it after the deposit of the

twentieth instrument of ratification or accession, the Convention shall enter into force on the thirtieth day after the date of the deposit of its own instrument of ratification or accession.

Article 28

1. The Secretary-General of the United Nations shall receive and circulate to all States the text of reservations made by States at the time of ratification or accession.

2. A reservation incompatible with the object and purpose of the present Convention shall not be permitted.

3. Reservations may be withdrawn at any time by notification to this effect addressed to the Secretary-General of the United Nations, who shall then inform all States thereof. Such notification shall take effect on the date on which it is received.

Article 29

1. Any dispute between two or more States Parties concerning the intepretation or application of the present Convention which is not settled by negotiation shall, at the request of one of them, be submitted to arbitration. If within six months from the date of the request for arbitration the parties are unable to agree on the organization of the arbitration, any one of those parties may refer the dispute to the International Court of Justice by request in conformity with the Statute of the Court.

2. Each State Party may at the time of signature or ratification of the present Convention or accession thereto declare that it does not consider itself bound by paragraph 1 of this article. The other States Parties shall not be bound by that paragraph with respect to any State Party which has made such a reservation.

3. Any State Party which has made a reservation in accordance with paragraph 2 of this article may at any time withdraw that reservation by notification to the Secretary-General of the United Nations.

Article 30

The present Convention, the Arabic, Chinese, English, French, Russian and Spanish texts of which are equally authentic, shall be deposited with the Secretary-General of the United Nations.

IN WITNESS WHEREOF the undersigned, duly authorized, have signed the present Convention.

Annex 2
It can be done

Incorporating women's concerns at all levels of development

Most people working today in development will agree that women's concerns have to be incorporated. The problem is how to do it.

The task demands a many-sided approach: national commitment, relevant policies, adequate resources, women's involvement. Even if all these factors were present, there would still be a need for permanent monitoring.

Development plans and projects, whether specifically targeting women or not, affect women's lives and are, in turn, affected by the organization of gender relations in a given society or group. That is why successful development activities require a thorough understanding of the way women and men perceive and act their social roles, and the ways these roles are changing under modernization.

Even then, this understanding per se does not guarantee women's concerns will be properly addressed. But there are tools to help us achieve this goal. The guidelines and checklists for women in development (WID) ensure the women's dimension is incorporated in national policies and in individual projects.*

WID guidelines and checklists, spawned by the United Nations Decade for Women (1976-1985), incorporate the new conceptual and analytical perspectives of over 15 years of WID thinking and research. A flexible instrument, they can help sharpen the ability of planners to gauge how their projects will differently affect women and men, and to understand their different needs.

Guidelines are broader and more general; they synthesize broad policy mandates concerning women. For example, what co-ordination exists between ministries, international agencies and women's groups? What mechanisms of communication between planners and project beneficiaries?

Checklists are more detailed and specific. Just as a pilot runs through a checklist before take-off, projects should be run through WID checklists on departure, during flight and after landing, that is, in their design, implementation and completion. Checklists function as detailed memory aids so that no aspect of the project will overlook women. For example, if training courses are given in the evening, can the women attend? If a water pump is installed, can the women repair it? If the women set up a co-operative, are there roads and transportation and markets for their products?

The evidence shows that often the failure of projects to reach women or their negative consequences stem from weaknesses in the initial stages. To avoid costly mistakes and omissions, the gender variable has to be incorporated early in the formulation of policies and the design of projects.

The set of guidelines and checklists in this supplement to INSTRAW News comes from a meeting (Dhaka, Bangladesh, 24-28 August 1986), jointly convened by the United Nations International Research and Training Institute for the Advancement of Women (INSTRAW), the Food and Agriculture Organization of the United Nations (FAO) and the Centre on Integrated Rural Development for Asia and the Pacific (CIRDAP). Participants from eleven Asian and South East Asian countries pooled their expertise to produce these guidelines and checklists oriented towards rural development.

The aim was to produce a prototype set, along broad basic lines, that could afterwards be expanded and adapted to different national realities. It is with the same aim that INSTRAW is now publishing a selection of these guidelines and checklists: to serve as a basis for our readers to develop their own. We urge you to use them, adapt them, and let us know your views and comments.

There is no easy approach to WID issues. The interrelationship of the productive and

*As part of its programme on training, INSTRAW is monitoring, evaluating and assessing the results of WID guidelines and checklists. The programme includes the compilation and dissemination of available material, development of prototype guidelines and checklists, and subsequent testing in selected countries.

reproductive activities of women, the interlinkages between the macro and the micro levels of the economy, the web of international and regional factors affecting the lives of women, collectively or as individuals, all these combine to weave the complex relationship of women and development that sometimes baffles planners.

And yet it can be done: Women's concerns can be incorporated at all levels. Women's potential can be tapped for development. It won't be easy; it won't happen overnight. To ensure that the women's dimension becomes a built-in component of development planning and programming will take a combination of research, training, information, activism and hard work. But there is simply no other way to conceive development these days: with women.

Selected guidelines

At the national level

1. Analysis of the situation of women
- An inter-regional data bank should store and disseminate socio-economic indicators and information on women, particularly on their contribution to agriculture, non-farm and household services.
- Women's contribution in farming and non-farming activities should be measured in statistics.

2. Political will for women's issues
- The national development objectives and stategies must incorporate women's concerns.
- National and political commitment must be translated into action.
- A watchdog regional pressure group composed of representatives of governmental and non-governmental organizations can assist in securing equality for women, e.g., repeal discriminatory laws, increase educational, training and employment opportunities, etc.
- Programmes of agricultural and rural development should have women as a specific target group, with substantial financial, material and human resources assigned.

3. A strategy to incorporate women
- Women must be actively involved at various levels of policy, planning, formulation and analysis, programme design, implementation, monitoring and evaluation at a sufficiently effective level.
- To strengthen women in their various economic roles, develop a package deal: training for transfer of technology; availability of credit; supply of inputs; storage; transportation; and marketing outlets with facilities.
- The national monitoring system should specifically take note of women.
- Develop specific training programmes to upgrade the skills of female planners in policy-making and programme planning.

At project level

1. Analysis of the local situation
- Analysis of the division of labour by gender in the indigenous production system will effectively identify the project beneficiaries.
- Plans for agrarian reforms, settlement of unoccupied lands, and the resettlement of the landless poor, refugees, and victims of natural disasters, should provide women with direct access to land.
- The introduction of labour-saving technology and/or re-organization of production structures shouldn't jeopardize women's gainful activities. If necessary, alternative job opportunites and activities should be provided.
- Provide women with direct access to land, water and other natural resources.
- Promote measures to increase women's labour contribution to agricultural production by reducing their workload in traditional household and farming systems.

2.1 Organizational set-up
- Suitable training programmes should assist women in developing skills to articulate their needs, assume leadership roles in local organizations, and negotiate over wages and working conditions.

• Promote collective action and organization by rural women; remove barriers for their participation in economic, social and political activities on an equal footing with men.
• Motivate, encourage and organize women's organizations to increase their bargaining power in negotiating over wages and working conditions at the grass roots level.

2.2 Vertical and horizontal linkages
• Linkages should be established between women's programmes of different line ministries and other agencies, including NGO's, to increase impact and avoid overlap.
• Complementary programmes of different Ministries (e.g., health, education, family planning) should be mutually reinforcing in order to improve women's socio-economic status.
• Channels of communication should convey the views, needs and priorities of rural women from grass-roots to policy level.

2.3 Resources
• In national plans for sanitation and reforestation, incorporate consideration for women's domestic use of water and fuel energy.
• Establish a mechanism to deliver agricultural inputs and support services catering to the special needs of women.
• Facilitate the introduction of appropriate technology for the pre-harvest, post-harvest and other domestic activities.
• Provide practical programmes to facilitate institutional credit for women's groups without collateral, and for the rental and purchase of land by women, individually or collectively.

2.4 Human resources development
• Establish special recruitment and training schemes to increase the number of women in training programmes for trainers at development agencies.
• Broaden the range of agricultural training and extension to support women's roles in all activities of agricultural production, processing, storage, preservation, transportation and marketing.
• Provide training in specific skills for income-generating, farm and off-farm activities for women.
• Provide training in nutrition, personal hygiene, environmental sanitation and household energy, among others, to improve the health of rural women and their families. Make agricultural and vocational training of girls a standard part of the curricula.

2.5 Monitoring and evaluation
• Monitor and evaluate girls' and women's enrollment in formal and non-formal education and training.
• Develop a built-in monitoring system to evaluate each factor (i.e. if the priorities established are being considered, the bargaining power of women's organization is increasing, resources are reaching women in time, etc.).

2.6 Reporting
• Establish a reporting system from the grass-roots to the policy level.
• Training on reporting and communication is essential for workers and women involved in the project.

Selected prototype checklists

Because of indigenous diversity within Asia and the Pacific region, the group formulated, for the national policy-planning level, a set of checklists encompassing major trends. At the project level, the checklists address women's concerns in agriculture, with emphasis on women's role in agro-based industry.

At the national policy-planning level

1. Analysis of the situation of women
• Are data on rural women's employment available? Are data disaggregated by sex in national censuses, surveys and studies?
• Do the national women's machineries arrange the collection of information on rural women, and its dissemination to all concerned agencies and organizations?

● Are socio-economic indicators on women suitable for different regional situations and for different target groups of women?

2. Consciousness, commitment and political will

● Are there any specific policy statements pertaining to women in agriculture and rural development? If not, a special chapter on WID must be included in the national development plans.

● What percentage of agricultural and rural development projects focus on women (poor, landless, destitute women, etc.)?

● What percentage of budgetary and other resources are allocated for WID in rural development, e.g., number of women extension officers, facilities and support services?

● Is there a mechanism to co-ordinate action for WID within and without the private sector?

3. Policy and mandate

● At what level are women involved in agriculture and rural development, e.g., planners, extension officers, rural leaders?

Are women targeted exclusively? What categories of women are involved: landless, etc.?

● Are women involved in policy formulation? At what levels?

● Is there a women's unit at the central planning organizations? Other national machineries?

Do these machineries have authority to monitor programmes of governmental and non-governmental agencies to ensure women's needs and concerns are met?

What programmes exist to organize rural women into self-help groups? Are these organizations represented and consulted in national and local planning?

● What constraints exist to involve women effectively in the planning process: legal; policies and development strategies; training and education; socio-cultural conditions (attitudinal, religious, etc.).

What steps are taken to remove these constraints: repeal and introduction of laws; appropriate training and education; increased awareness of the importance of women's contribution to development.

4. Strategies to incorporate women

● Do women have access to natural resources such as land, water, etc.?

Are credit facilities for women available through banks or co-operatives? Can women have access as heads of families or as wives?

Can women readily join group organizations such as workers' groups, co-operatives, etc.?

Can they easily obtain inputs such as fertilizers, seeds, chemicals, etc.?

● What training is available for women in: awareness; skills; leadership, etc.

At project level

Because the majority of countries in the Asia-Pacific region are mainly oriented towards agriculture, the group gave priority to agro-based industry that could employ a large number of women.

In rural planning, the initial stages of formulating a project are crucial. From experience, it has been repeatedly observed that, if thoroughly conducted, a feasibility study to find out the economic viability of the project can avoid many mistakes.

1. Establishment of priorities through analysis of local situation and identification of target groups

● Has a feasibility study been done to identify the following: total production of agricultural produce; estimates of surplus production and price; proportion of women among the producers; various items which can be produced, the technologies available, and women's participation in the proposed production and techniques; if women have the necessary skills to use these technologies or would they require training; market outlets for products (local, national or export); marketing services and facilities, existing or to be arranged; training required, to be provided locally or elsewhere; availability of credit and any constraints or preconditions concerning women; arrangements to remove these; proposed participation of women in project management, and management training required; activities of the project that can be conducted in the houses of women workers and then centrally processed; support services available or proposed for child care, health care and transportation; organizational

arrangements for marketing and systematic upgrading of technology; mode of organizing women to improve their bargaining power; projections for the project to reach self-reliance and for future activities for women's employment; identification of categories of women who will benefit from the project.
- What is the economic viability of the project? Socio-economic condition of women in the selected project area can be ascertained from the following data: age distribution; education attainment; marital status; age and sex distribution of population; type of social hierarchy; women's activities; religion.

In the public programme for the distribution of land or assets, are there instructions to allocate a percentage to landless and poor households headed by women, or for joint allotment to the male and female members of families participating in the project?

Has a study identified the technologies used or proposed for agriculture? Has a study examined the detrimental effects on women in terms of labour displacement, special health hazards and increased work burden? If so, measures proposed: alternative employment, labour and time-saving devices for water, sanitation, fuel and fodder.

Are there women's groups, institutions, co-operatives functioning? How many? How many women are involved?

Has the following been identified and quantified? – total amount and type of agricultural production; number of women involved in agriculture; categories of women involved in agriculture (married, divorced, widowed, unmarried, landless, poor).
- What are women's land rights and access to water and other land resources – lease, freehold, inheritance. Is there legislation? Are there social or religious taboos?
- What are the levels of technology used? Mechanization, animal draught, manual, type of crops, variety of crops. Is the technology feasible? Do women have access to and use of technology? What is the impact of new technologies, e.g., facilitating work, displacing women? Are there alternative types of production: agriculture-crops; livestock; silviculture; apiculture? What post harvest technology is needed?

What would be the degree of women's participation in: decision making, management, planting, weeding, harvesting, processing, storage marketing?
- Availability and access of inputs to women: credit, labour, water, fertilizers and seeds.
- Is expertise among women available in: planning, decision-making, management, leadership, processing, technical, marketing?
- Are there arrangements to remove the legal, socio-cultural constraints?
- Who are the beneficiaries (as in categories involved in agriculture)?

2. Organizational set-up
- Are women informed about project feasibility regarding: inputs; credit; marketing infrastructure; legislation and regulations; concerning the project activities; employment conditions; implementing agencies; benefits?
- Have women at all levels been involved in the project preparation?
- Were the target group of women involved?
- What is the mechanism for implementation, monitoring, etc., of the project at local, regional and national levels?
- Is there a project committee?; what is the membership (government, NGOs and target group)?
- How have women been organized in formal/non-formal groups to increase their management efficiency and improve their bargaining power? Ascertain the following: a set of working guidelines for such organizations; linkages with any higher level organizations that can ensure access to inputs and markets; links with programmes of line ministries/agencies relevant to the project.

3. Communication and co-ordination
- What type of research is being conducted to generate up-to-date information on women?
- How is this information disseminated? To whom?
- What are the mechanisms for monitoring its out-reach to women in various locations, its effectiveness and use?
- What steps have been taken to set up a committee for co-ordination of work among agencies at different levels?

4. Human resources development
- What number and percentage of women are recruited as extension workers?
- Are women included in the training of trainers?
- Does the curriculum of training extension and rural development workers contain a women's component?
- What are the existing training programmes in production skills for women in income-generating activities, e.g., training in management, marketing, etc.
- Is training provided near their homes or hostel facilities provided?

5. Monitoring and evaluation
- Has the project identified the aspects to be monitored and the frequency? Indicators need to be developed.
- Does the project include a midterm or annual evaluation?
- What mechanism has been built into the project for corrective action on the basis of evaluation?
- Has a reporting system with formats, period and other contents been established?

Annex 3

Organizations that have agreed to implement the system-wide medium-term plan for women and development

Programme and subprogramme	Level of responsibility	
	Major	Supporting
1. *Elimination of legal and attitudinal forms of discrimination*		
1.1 International standards	United Nations (UNOV, UNHCR), ILO	United Nations (DTCD), UNESCO
1.2 Promoting more positive attitudes towards the role of women in development	United Nations (UNOV, DPI, ESCAP, ECA, ESCWA), UNESCO, INSTRAW, UNDP, UNIFEM	United Nations (WFC, UNEP), UNFPA, UNICEF, ILO, FAO, WHO, WFP, World Bank, UNIDO, IFAD
2. *Access to productive resources, income and development*		
2.1 Overall trends and policies in women's employment	ILO, UNIFEM, United Nations (ESCAP, ECA, ESCWA)	UNIDO, United Nations (DIESA, DTCD, ECLAC, ECE, UNCTAD), FAO, INSTRAW, UNDP, World Bank
2.2 Vocational training and training on women and development	ILO, INSTRAW, United Nations (DTCD, CSTD, UNRWA, ECA, ESCWA), UNESCO, UNIFEM, WHO	United Nations (Habitat, UNCTAD, UNHCR, UNEP), UNDP, FAO, UNIDO, WFP, UNFPA
2.3 Food and agriculture	FAO, IFAD, UNIFEM, WFP, United Nations (ECA, UNEP), World Bank	UNDP, United Nations (ESCAP, UNCTAD, CSTD, WFC, UNHCR, DTCD), UNICEF, ILO, UNIDO
2.4 Industry	UNIDO, UNIFEM, United Nations (ESCAP, ECA, ESCWA, UNEP)	United Nations (DIESA, CSTD, Habitat, UNCTAD), ILO, FAO, UNDP
2.5 Entrepreneurship and access to credit	UNIFEM, United Nations (DIESA, DTCD, ECA), FAO	United Nations (ESCAP, ECE, UNCTAD), ILO, ITC, UNIDO, WFP, UNDP, UNICEF
2.6 Informal sector	ILO, INSTRAW, UNIFEM, United Nations (Habitat, DTCD, ESCAP, ECA, ESCWA), WFP	United Nations (ECE, UNCTAD, UNHCR, UNRWA), UNFPA, UNIDO, FAO, IFAD, UNESCO
3. *Access to services*		
3.1 Health, nutrition and family planning	WHO, UNFPA, UNICEF, FAO, WFP, IFAD, World Bank, United Nations (ECLAC, UNRWA)	United Nations (DTCD, WFC, UNHCR, UNEP, UNCTAD), ILO, UNIFEM

| Programme and subprogramme | Level of responsibility | |
	Major	Supporting
3.2 Literacy and education	UNESCO, UNICEF	United Nations (CSTD, UNCTAD, UNHCR, UNRWA), UNFPA, World Bank, FAO, WFP
3.3 Housing, settlement, water, energy and transport	United Nations (ECA, Habitat, UNEP, UNRWA, DTCD, DIESA), FAO, WFP, UNICEF, INSTRAW, IFAD, UNIFEM, UNDP	United Nations (UNCTAD, CSTD, UNHCR), ILO, UNESCO, WHO
3.4 Other social infrastructure and support services	United Nations (UNOV, DIESA, UNRWA, ESCAP, ESCWA, ECA), ILO, WHO, UNICEF, UNESCO, UNIFEM	WFP, UNIDO, United Nations (UNCTAD, UNHCR), FAO
4. *Decision-making*		
4.1 Participation in management and decision-making	United Nations (UNOV, OHRM, DTCD, ESCWA, ECA, ESCAP), INSTRAW, ILO, UNIFEM, UNFPA	United Nations (UNEP, UNHCR), UNDP, WHO, UNIDO, UNESCO, FAO
4.2 Participation in groups, associations, co-operatives, trade unions and other non-governmental organizations	ILO, INSTRAW, UNIFEM, United Nations (UNOV, DIESA), UNIDO, FAO, WHO, UNDP, UNFPA, UNICEF	United Nations (ESCAP, ECLAC, UNEP, UNHCR), WFP
5. *Improving means of international action*		
5.1 Development of statistics and indicators	United Nations (DIESA, DTCD, ECLAC, ESCWA, ESCAP), ILO, FAO, INSTRAW, UNESCO	UNFPA, United Nations (ECA, Habitat, UNCTAD), World Bank, WHO, UNIDO
5.2 Information and dissemination	United Nations (DPI, UNOV, UNEP, ESCWA, ECA, ESCAP, ECLAC), INSTRAW, ILO, FAO, UNESCO	WFP, UNFPA, UNIFEM, United Nations (DTCD, UNHCR)
5.3 Research, policy analysis and dissemination	United Nations (UNOV, DIESA, DPI, ECLAC, ESCAP, ECA, ESCWA), INSTRAW, ILO, UNIFEM, UNESCO	FAO, UNFPA, UNIDO, World Bank, United Nations (UNCTAD, DTCD, Habitat, UNHCR), UNDP
5.4 Technical co-operation, training and advisory services	UNDP, United Nations (DTCD, ECLAC), UNIFEM, ILO, FAO, WHO, UNIDO, INSTRAW, UNESCO	UNFPA, World Bank, IMO, United Nations (Habitat, ESCAP, UNCTAD, UNEP, UNHCR), WFP
5.5 Science and technology	United Nations (CSTD, UNCTAD, ECA), INSTRAW, ILO, UNIDO, FAO, WHO	UNESCO, UNDP

Programme and subprogramme	Level of responsibility	
	Major	Supporting
6. *Comprehensive approaches to women and development*		
6.1 Analysis of the interrelationship of factors affecting women and development	United Nations (UNOV, DIESA, ESCWA, ECA, ESCAP, ECLAC, UNEP), INSTRAW, UNIFEM	ILO, FAO, WHO, UNESCO, UNIDO, UNFPA, World Bank, WFP, United Nations (UNCTAD, UNHCR, UNEP), UNDP, UNICEF
6.2 Monitoring and review and appraisal of basic policy guidelines and national experience	United Nations (UNOV, DIESA, ESCWA, ESCAP, ECA, ECLAC), INSTRAW, UNIFEM	UNFPA, ILO, FAO, UNESCO, WHO, UNIDO, WFP, United Nations (DTCD, UNHCR), IFAD
6.3 Strengthening national machineries and mechanisms for planning and policy-making	United Nations (UNOV, DTCD, ECA, ESCAP, ECLAC, ESCWA, UNEP), UNIFEM, INSTRAW, UNFPA	FAO, United Nations (WFC)
6.4 Co-ordinating a system-wide approach to women and development	United Nations system	

Annex 4
Relevant world conferences

1. United Nations Conference on the Human Environment, Stockholm — 3-16 June 1972
2. United Nations World Population Conference, Bucharest — 19-30 August 1974
3. World Food Conference, Rome — 5-16 Nov 1974
4. World Conference of the International Women's Year, Mexico City — 19 June-2 July 1975
5. HABITAT: United Nations Conference on Human Settlements, Vancouver — 31 May-11 June 1976
6. Tripartite World Conference on Employment, Income Distribution Social Progress and the International Division of Labour, Geneva — June 1976
7. Conference on Economic Co-operation among Developing Countries, Mexico — 13-22 Sept 1976
8. United Nations Water Conference, Mar del Plata — 14-25 March 1977
9. United Nations Conference on Desertification, Nairobi — 29 Aug-9 Sept 1977
10. World Conference to Combat Racism and Racial Discrimination, Geneva — 14-25 August 1978
11. United Nations Conference on Technical Co-operation among Developing Countries, Buenos Aires — 30 Aug-12 Sept 1978
12. Primary Health Care Conference, Alma Ata — September 1978
13. World Conference on Agrarian Reform and Rural Development, Rome — 12-20 July 1979
14. United Nations Conference on Science and Technology for Development, Vienna — 20-31 August 1979
15. World Conference of the United Nations Decade for Women, Copenhagen — 14-30 July 1980
16. United Nations Conference on New and Renewable Sources of Energy, Nairobi — 10-21 August 1981
17. United Nations Conference on the Least Developed Countries, Paris — 1-14 September 1981
18. World Conference to Review and Appraise the Achievements of the UN Decade for Women, Nairobi — 15-26 July 1985
19. International Conference on the Relationship between Disarmament and Development, New York — 24 Aug-11 Sept 1987
20. United Nations Conference on Environment and Development, Brazil — June 1992

Annex 5

A practical guide:
How to prepare a resolution for a UN conference

Who can propose resolutions or amendments at UN conferences?

As the UN System is an intergovernmental system only government delegations are entitled to propose resolutions. There are two ways in which non-governmental groups can get their draft resolution proposed:

• to work with their own national authorities in charge of the preparations for the conference, and to try to persuade them to take up the question. If the initiator can provide a well-prepared draft of the resolution it is easier to persuade those concerned. Best of all, the initiator may have a chance to become an advisory member of her country's delegation.

• to attend the conference as an NGO observer, participant in the NGO Forum, or in any available context. When physically present one can contact delegates of various countries and try to persuade them to take up the proposed resolution. In such negotiations a well-prepared draft resolution is essential.

The preparatory work

Careful preparation is the precondition for an attempt to get a resolution adopted by any UN body. A draft resolution showing expertise in the subject matter and in procedure has the best chance of being adopted. To begin preparation of a draft resolution, one should:

• be clear about the nature and level of the conference or meeting, in order to define what kind of resolution can come under consideration (one cannot propose a project resolution in a policy-making body, or vice versa);

• study the previous resolutions of the organ or organization on the same subject, in order to become acquainted with what has been said before and the formulations and language of this particular body;

• if there are no previous resolutions of this body on the subject, one should study resolutions of corresponding organs or organizations on the issue;

• resolutions and decisions of other bodies on the subject should be studied anyway, in order to be able to refer to those of relevance in the draft resolution to be prepared;

• in the case of a specific body – such as a world conference – one should study the main documentation, and the rules of procedure of conferences of this type, in order to find out where the subject could fit in and in what form (maybe an addition, or amendment, instead of a resolution).

On the basis of these studies one can draft a preliminary text for the proposal.

Form of the proposal

The structure of the resolution usually consists of:

• the introductory or preambular part, consisting of paragraphs which may present some strong basic arguments for the subject and in which reference can be made to other relevant resolutions of the UN System;

• the operative part, consisting of the provisions concerning what is urged to be done in the matter and tasks for various organs or bodies, upon which obligations may be placed (depending on the level and nature of the decision-making body in question).

It is always useful to consult experts or interested parties, including delegates and members of the UN secretariat, about the preliminary draft, so that a new, improved draft can be formulated.

Case study No. 1

Addendum 1 to this Annex is the resolution on "Women, science and technology" of the UN conference on Science and Technology for Development, held in Vienna in 1979.

This UNCSTD resolution was prepared together by three 'like-minded' women during the conference itself in Vienna. Two were there as members of their national delegations (Norway and Finland). They also consulted some professional diplomats during the process.

The initiative for the separate resolution was taken as an alternative to efforts being made to obtain amendments to the conference document itself, which seemed to bring no results. When the draft resolution was presented to different delegations, however, it received a positive response from most of them, and within two days there were already about a dozen co-sponsors. Austria as host country signed the resolution as the first of the sponsors. Then it was given to the secretariat to be printed as an official document for distribution to all delegations.

Since the resolution was general in character it was taken up in plenary rather than in any of the Commissions. It was included as a special item on the agenda for the final plenary session, where it was introduced by the Ambassador of Tanzania and adopted unanimously. It addresses itself to all relevant agents in the matter, to member states, all organs, organizations and other bodies of the UN System, and the new intergovernmental Committee on Science and Technology for Development. A key point in the resolution is the obligation placed upon the new Committee "to include in its annual reports a review on the progress made concerning the implementation of the tenets of the present resolution". These reports are especially important because through them the member governments can ensure implementation of the resolution, so that it does not remain a dead letter.

Case study No. 2

The resolution on Women and Industrialization adopted at the Third General Conference of the UN Industrial Development Organization (UNIDO) in 1980 was first drafted in Finland and introduced to the Finnish delegation to UNIDO III. A strong argument in this connection was that Finland had already, in 1975, initiated a resolution on women at the UNIDO Board Meeting, where it was adopted unanimously; so it was felt that Finland should continue to work on the issue and ensure that it is given due regard in the future.

UNIDO III was held in order to draw the outline for industrial development for the rest of the century. It was therefore important to propose a resolution which would oblige the Executive Director of UNIDO to give enough attention, in appropriate ways, to the interests and views of women in all of the organization's activities. The Finnish delegation took up the question with their Nordic colleagues in one of their pre-conference meetings, with a view to a possible joint Nordic venture in this matter; the response was positive.

At the Conference the draft resolution was submitted by the Nordic countries and co-sponsored by ten other countries from all regions and various political groups. Finally this resolution became almost the only thing upon which UNIDO III was able to agree unanimously. (And the Finnish delegation did its job with a 100% male crew!)

In this resolution one might note the operative paragraph obliging the Director-General of the Organization to proceed step-by-step in actions to promote the aims of the resolution, and to report upon these actions in all appropriate connections so that member governments can monitor the implementation of the recommendations (see Addendum 2 to this Annex).

And so?

What is the importance of UN resolutions and recommendations? When a resolution has been adopted does it work automatically? The answer is no; the resolution is but the first step in the process of achieving the aims expressed in it. The decisive importance lies in the follow-up of the resolution in member states and by the member governments.

In the member states all those interested in the advancement of women should keep up-to-date concerning relevant resolutions and recommendations adopted by different organs and organizations. They should follow up keenly, to see how their government is implementing the resolutions and, if it is not, make it known in public and mobilize the people to make it clear that they expect more of the government. This is the only way to guarantee that the resolution will become more than a piece of paper.

In order to follow the fulfilment by the UN System itself of the obligations addressed to them, the interested groups in each country should enquire through appropriate channels about reports and other information with regard to the provisions concerned and their implementation. Then they should contact national authorities and delegations as to follow-up by delegations to the respective UN bodies. If member states don't see to it, UN bodies may forget their obligations too.

This follow-up activity is as important in connection with the Nairobi Forward-looking Strategies, and the Convention on the Elimination of All Forms of Discrimination against

Women, as it is in the case of any other resolution or recommendation concerning women. Only in this way can we really make things happen.

United Nations Conference on Science and Technology for Development

(Vienna, Austria, August 1979)

Austria, Australia, Denmark, Ethiopia, Finland, Hungary, Jamaica, Norway, Mongolia, Papua New Guinea, Somalia, Sweden, Thailand, United Republic of Tanzania, United States of America and Viet Nam:
draft resolution

Women, science and technology

The United Nations Conference on Science and Technology for Development,

Mindful that the International Women's Decade was proclaimed in order to draw attention to the problems faced by women in their daily lives and to stimulate recognition at the national and international levels of the loss experienced where women, accounting for half of the world's adult population, are not given equal opportunity to contribute fully to national development,

Recalling General Assembly resolutions 3342 (XXIX) of 17 December 1974 and 3524 (XXX) of 15 December 1975 on the integration of women in development, in which the Assembly urged Governments to give sustained attention to the integration of women in the planning, formulation, design and implementation of development projects and programmes, as well as General Assembly resolution 33/184 of 29 January 1979, on importance of the improvement of the status and role of women in education and in the economic and social fields for the achievement of the equality of women with men,

Recalling the relevant proposals of the World Plan of Action for the Implementation of the Objectives of the International Women's Year adopted at the Conference of the International Women's Year held at Mexico City, the World Population Plan of action and the World Food Conference, as well as the World Conference on Agrarian reform and Rural Development on the integration of women in development,

Noting the importance accorded to the integration of women in development by the Governing Council of the United Nations Development Programme as its nineteenth session and at the ninth session of the Industrial Development Board of the United Nations Industrial Development Organization,

Mindful that the Economic Commission for Africa Training and Research Centre for Women, the Economic and Social Commission for Asia and the Pacific, the United Nations Conference on Trade and Development, the United Nations Children's Fund, the International Labour Organization, the United Nations Development Programme, the Food and Agriculture Organization of the United Nations, the United Nations Educational, Scientific and Cultural Organization and the World Bank have planned activities and studies concerning technological development in order to enhance women's contribution to economic life,

Recalling Economic and Social Council resolution 1978/34 of 5 May 1978 on women in development and international conferences, in which the Council urged all Governments to ensure that the topic of women and development be included within the substantive discussions of the Conference, including the United Nations Conference on Science and Technology for Development,

Recognizing the importance of the present quantity and quality of the contribution of women, and its potential value where fully and appropriately utilized and developed, for the well-being and wealth of their families and societies as a whole,

1. *Invites* Member States to facilitate:

(*a*) The equal distribution of the benefits of scientific and technological development and its application to men and women in society;

(*b*) The participation of women in the decision making process related to science and technology, including planning and setting priorities for research and development and in the choice, acquisition, adaptation, innovation, and application of science and technology for development;

(*c*) The equal access for women and men to scientific and technological training and to the respective professional careers;

2. *Recommends* that all organs, organizations and other bodies of the United Nations system related to science and technology should:

(*a*) Continually review the impact of their programmes and activities on women;

(*b*) Promote the full participation of women in planning and implementation of their programmes;

3. *Invites* the proposed intergovernmental Committee on Science and Technology for Development:

(*a*) To give due regard to the perspectives and interests of women in all its recommendations, programmes and actions;

(*b*) To include in its annual reports a review of the progress made concerning the implementation of the tenets of the present resolution;

4. *Recommends* to the forthcoming World Conference of the United Nations Decade for Women: Equality, Development and Peace, scheduled to be held in 1980, to give due consideration to the relationships between women, science, technology and development.

1. Resolution on Women and Industrialization

273. At the 21st plenary meeting, on 9 February 1980, the representative of Finland introduced a draft resolution on "Women and Industrialization" (ID/CONF.4/L.2) submitted by Denmark, Finland, Norway and Sweden and co-sponsored by Hungary, India, Mexico, Netherlands, Peru, Philippines, Portugal, Tunisia, the United Republic of Tanzania and Yugoslavia.

274. At the same meeting, the Conference adopted the resolution by consensus. The resolution, as adopted (ID/CONF.4/RES. 1), reads as follows:

'*The Third General Conference of the United Nations Industrial Development Organization,*

'*Mindful* that the United Nations Decade for Women was proclaimed to draw attention to the problems faced by women in their daily lives and to stimulate recognition at the national and international levels of the loss experienced where women, accounting for half of the world's adult population, are not given equal opportunity to contribute fully to national development,

'*Recalling* the results of the World Conference of the International Women's Year, held at Mexico City, from 19 June to 2 July 1975,

'*Recalling also* General Assembly resolutions 3342 (XXIX) of 17 December 1974 on women in development, and 3524 (XXX) of 15 December 1975 on measures for the integration of women in development, in which the General Assembly urged Governments to give sustained attention to the integration of women in the planning, formulation, design and implementation of development projects and programmes,

'*Further recalling* the provisions of the Lima Declaration and Plan of Action on Industrial Development and Co-operation concerning the full integration of women in social and economic activities and, in particular, in the industrialization process, on the basis of equal rights,

'*Recalling in particular* Industrial Development Board resolution 44 (IX) of 25 April 1975 on the integration of women in development,

'*Taking into consideration* the recommendations of the Preparatory Meeting on the Role of women in Industrialization in Developing Countries, held in Vienna from 6 to 10 November 1978,

'*Taking also into consideration* resolution 2 on women, science and technology, adopted by the United Nations Conference on Science and Technology for Development on 31 August 1979,

'*Having considered* in response to the request contained in General Assembly resolution 34/204 of 19 December 1979 on effective mobilization and integration of women in development, *inter alia*:

(*a*) The impact of new technology and the deployment of modern industries on women's traditional skills and occupations which may be endangered, and

(*b*) The indentification of ways and means of enhancing and facilitating the equal participation of women in industrial development, in both rural and urban areas,

'*Bearing in mind* the responsibility of the United Nations Industrial Development

Organization to develop concrete programmes aimed at integrating women in the industrialization process of developing countries in accordance with the decision taken by the Industrial Development Board, at is thirteenth session,

'*Mindful* that further discussions on the effective integration of women in development, and in particular on the sub theme 'Employment, Education and Health', will take place at the World Conference of the United Nations Decade for Women: Equality, Development and Peace to be held in Copenhagen in 1980,

'1. *Emphasizes* that the integration and participation of women at all levels in the industrialization process is a vital prerequisite for balanced and equitable development;

'2. *Calls on* all Governments to seek to promote the involvement and integration of women in the industrial development and to take measures to eliminate discriminatory attitudes and practices hampering the effective participation of women in the development process;

'3. *Stresses* the essential role the United Nations Industrial Development Organization has to play in the integration of women in industrial development;

'4. *Welcomes* as a first step the establishment of an Interdivisional Working Group on Integration of Women in Industrial Development within the Secretariat of the United Nations Industrial Development Organization to deal with and co-ordinate activities related to the integration of women in development;

'5. *Expresses the desire* that the Interdivisional Working Group make rapid progress in its work;

'6. *Urges* the Executive Director of the United Nations Industrial Development Organization to take further measures to facilitate the work of the Interdivisional Working Group in fulfilling its mandate and to submit to the Industrial Development Board, at its fourteenth session, a preliminary progress report;

'7. *Requests* the Executive Director of the United Nations Industrial Development Organization to report on the impact of the industrialization process on women in forthcoming issues of the *Industrial Development Survey* and in future monitoring of the implementation of the Lima Declaration and Plan of Action;

'8. *Requests also* the Executive Director of the United Nations Industrial Development Organization to assist Governments, upon request, in developing data collection systems and reporting methods to provide information – *inter alia*, for the analyses of the Executive Director – on the integration of women in industrial development, keeping in mind such relevant aspects as employment, training, access to jobs and remuneration;

'9. *Further requests* the Executive Director of the United Nations Industrial Development Organization to provide data on participation of women in the activities of the Organization – such as training, fellowship programmes, seminars and courses – in his future *Annual Reports* and other relevant reports;

'10. *Invites* the Executive Director of the United Nations Industrial Development Organization to undertake urgently the studies requested by the Industrial Development Board, at its thirteenth session, on:

(*a*) The selected industries, such as electronics, food processing, and pharmaceutical and textile industries, and their impact on women, and

(*b*) The possible impact of industrial redeployment on women,

and to submit the reports on these studies to the Industrial Development Board at its fourteenth session;

'11. *Further invites* the Executive Director of the United Nations Industrial Development Organization, in implementing the Lima Declaration and Plan of Action:

(*a*) To keep under constant review the impact of these decisions on women,

(*b*) To promote the participation of men and women alike in planning and decision-making, both in their own countries and at the international level, as well as in the carrying out of measures to promote industrialization in developing countries, and

(*c*) To formulate and implement the industrialization programmes of the Organization with the full participation of men and women alike;

'12. *Recommends* that the Executive Director of the United Nations Industrial Development Organization take measures to ensure the more effective participation of women in decision- and policy-making processes within the Secretariat of the United Nations Industrial Development Organization and in the field, in accordance with the appropriate resolutions of the General Assembly and other bodies;

'13. *Invites* the Executive Director of the United Nations Industrial Development Organization to report on the integration and participation of women in the process of industrial development to the World Conference of the United Nations Decade for Women: Equality, Development and Peace, to be held in Copenhagen in 1980;

'14. *Requests* the Executive Director of the United Nations Industrial Development Organization to report on the progress achieved in the implementation of the present resolution to the Industrial Development Board at its fifteenth session.'

Annex 6
Relevant international instruments

1. United Nations

A. General instruments
Charter of the United Nations.
Universal Declaration of Human Rights (1948).
International Covenant on Economic, Social and Cultural Rights (1966).
International Covenant on Civil and Political Rights and Optional Protocol (1966).
Supplementary Convention on the Abolition of Slavery, the Slave Trade, and Institutions and Practices Similar to Slavery (1956).
International Convention on the Elimination of All Forms of Racial Discrimination (1965).
Declaration on Social Progress and Development (1969).
World Population Plan of Action (1974).
Programme of Action on the Establishment of a New International Economic Order (1974).
Charter of Economic Rights and Duties of States (1974).
International Development Strategy for the Third United Nations Development Decade (1980).

B. Instruments relating specifically to the status of women
Convention for the Suppression of the Traffic in Persons and of the Exploitation of the Prostitution of Others (1949).
Convention of the Political Rights of Women (1952).
Convention on the Nationality of Married Women (1957).
Convention and Recommendation on Consent to Marriage , Minimum Age for Marriage and Registration of Marriages (1962 and 1965).
Declaration on the Elimination of Discrimination against Women (1967).
Programme of concerted international action for the Advancement of Women (1970).
Declaration of Mexico, World Plan of Action (1975).
Convention on the Elimination of All Forms of Discrimination against Women (1979).
Nairobi Forward-looking Strategies for the Advancement of Women (1985).

2. Specialized agency instruments

A: International Labour Organization
Convention concerning the employment of women on underground work in mines of all kinds, No. 45 (1935).
Convention concerning night work of women employed in industry (revised), No. 89 (1948).
Convention concerning equal remuneration for men and women workers for work of equal value, No. 100 (1951), and Recommendation No. 90 (1951).
Convention concerning minimum standards of social security, No. 102 (1952).
Convention concerning maternity protection (revised) No. 103 (1952); and Recommendation No. 95 (1952).
Convention concerning discrimination in respect of employment and occupation, No. 111 (1958); and Recommendation No. 111 (1958).
Convention concerning employment policy, No. 122 (1964); and Recommendation No. 122 (1964).
Recommendation concerning vocational training, No. 117 (1962).
Recommendation concerning the employment of women with family responsibiliies, No. 123 (1965).
Convention concerning Equal Opportunities and Equal Treatment for Men and Women Workers. Workers with Family Responsibilities No. 156 (1981).

B: United Nations Educational, Scientific and Cultural Organization (Unesco)
Convention against Discrimination in Education (1960).
Protocol instituting a Conciliation and Good Offices Commission to be responsible for seeking a settlement of any disputes which may arise between States Parties to the Convention against Discrimination in Education (1962).

Annex 7
Where to ask for more information:

The Division for the Advancement of Women, Centre for Social Development and Humanitarian Affairs.
Vienna International Centre,
P.O. Box 500, A-1400, Vienna, Austria.

UN/NGLS (Non-Governmental Liaison Service), Palais des Nations,
CH-1211 Geneva 10, Switzerland.

Centre for Human Rights, (Questions Concerning Women), United Nations Office at Geneva, Palais des Nations,
CH-1211 Geneva 10, Switzerland.

International Research and Training Institute for the Advancement of Women (INSTRAW),
P.O. Box 21747,
Santo Domingo,
Dominican Republic.

Department of Public Information,
United Nations,
New York, NY 10017, USA.

Women's Indicators and Statistics Dept. of International Economic and Social Affairs,
United Nations,
New York, NY 10017, USA.

and from United Nations Information Centres worldwide:

United Nations Centre for Human Settlements (HABITAT),
Focal Point for Women,
P.O. Box 30030, Nairobi, Kenya.

The United Nations Development Fund for Women (UNIFEM),
304 East 45th Street, Room 1106,
New York, NY 10017, USA.

United Nations Development Programme (UNDP),
Division for Women's Programmes,
One UN Plaza,
New York, NY 10017, USA.

United Nations Educational, Scientific and Cultural Organization (UNESCO),
Co-ordinator of Programmes Relating to the Status of Women,
Bureau of Studies and Programming,
7 Place de Fontenoy,
75700 Paris, France.

United Nations Environment Programme (UNEP),
P.O. Box 30552, Nairobi, Kenya.

United Nations Industrial Development Organization (UNIDO),
Unit for the Integration of Women in Industrial Development,
Department for Programme and Project Development,
P.O. Box 300, A-1400 Vienna, Austria.

The World Bank,
Women in Development Division,
1818 H Street, NW,
Washington, DC 20433, USA.

Regional programmes:
United Nations Economic Commission for Africa (ECA),
African Training and Research Centre for Women,
P.O. Box 3001, Addis Ababa, Ethiopia.

United Nations Economic and Social Commission for Western Asia (ESCWA),
Women's Programme Officer,
Social Development and Population Division,
P.O. Box 27, Baghdad, Iraq.

United Nations Economic Commission for Latin America and the Caribbean (ECLAC),
Unit for the Integration of Women into Development,
Edificio Naciones Unidas,
Avenida Dag Hammarskjöld,
Casilla 179-D,
Santiago, Chile.

ECLAC Subregional Office for the Caribbean,
Women in Development,
P.O. Box 1113,
Port-of-Spain, Trinidad and Tobago,

United Nations Regional Commission for Europe (ECE),
Focal Point for Women,
Palais des Nations,
1211 Geneva 10, Switzerland.

For the status of women at the United Nations:
The Co-ordinator for the Improvement of the Status of Women in the United Nations,
Office of Human Resources Management,
United Nations, New York, NY 10017, USA.

For films, photos, radio and print material on women:

United Nations Information Service,
Palais des Nations,
CH-1211 Geneva 10,
Switzerland.

Project Manager, Women's Issues,
Communications and Project Management Service, DPI,
United Nations, New York.

Index